CONTENTS

GAUGAU WATA ガゥガゥわー太
BOW WOW WATA
Volume 1
ART and STORY:
UMEKAWA KAZUMI

CHAPTER 1: MEET WATA

TO ALL ANIMALS:
DISCUSS YOUR PROBLEMS WITH US!
YASHIRO ANIMAL CLINIC

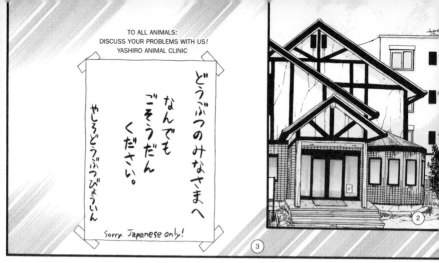

どうぶつのみなさまへ
なんでもごそうだんください。
やしろどうぶつびょういん

Sorry. Japanese only!

WHAT'S THIS? UH-HUH... *WHAT?*
THE DOCTOR AT THIS CLINIC CAN TALK TO ANIMALS?
I'VE BEEN WONDERING ABOUT THIS POSTER, TOO. I BET IT'S A FLUKE.

おほほ
O-HO HO...
I GUESS EVEN HOSPITALS WILL DO ANYTHING FOR BUSINESS THESE DAYS.
WELL, WE ARE IN A RECESSION... BUT TALK TO ANIMALS?
がしっ!
GRAB!

GOTCHA!

チャ

TOSS

MEOW

MEOW

MEOW

MEOW TO SOMEONE WHO UNDERSTANDS, 'CAUSE I DON'T.

MEOW

MEOW

MEOW

MEOW

THEY'RE THANKING YOU.
CAN YOU NOT TELL BY THE EXPRESSION ON THEIR FACES?
MEOW
MEOW
TAKE CARE, EVERYONE. AND SAT-CHAN, PLEASE TRY NOT TO WANDER SO FAR AWAY FROM HOME!
HEY, DAD!

I DON'T CARE IF YOU WANNA HELP ANIMALS, BUT WHY'D YOU MAKE *ME* LOOK FOR THAT CAT'S KITTENS? WHY COULDN'T *YOU* DO IT!?
IT COULD NOT BE HELPED. I CANNOT LEAVE THE CLINIC UNATTENDED.
ANYWAY, WE MUST CLEAN THOSE CUTS OF YOURS BEFORE THEY GET INFECTED.
キレイにしとかないと

IT IS STILL NOT TOO LATE FOR YOU TO BECOME A GREAT ANIMAL COUNSELOR IF YOU START NOW!
I'M *NOT* GONNA BE A VET, DAD!

HOW MANY TIMES DO I HAVE TO SAY IT?
I DON'T UNDERSTAND ANIMAL TALK LIKE YOU DO!
ON TOP OF THAT, I DON'T WANNA BE A VET!
I'M GONNA DO WHAT *I* WANNA DO!

めそめそ
(SNIFFLE, SNIFFLE)
HONEY, TASUKE IS A BAD BOY.
THANKS TO *YOU*.

(SIGH)
I DON'T SUPPOSE THERE IS ANY WAY YOU WILL COME TO UNDERSTAND ANIMAL TALK ANY TIME SOON.
HEY, CUT IT OUT! I DON'T NOW AND I'LL NEVER BE ABLE TO! I'M *HUMAN!*

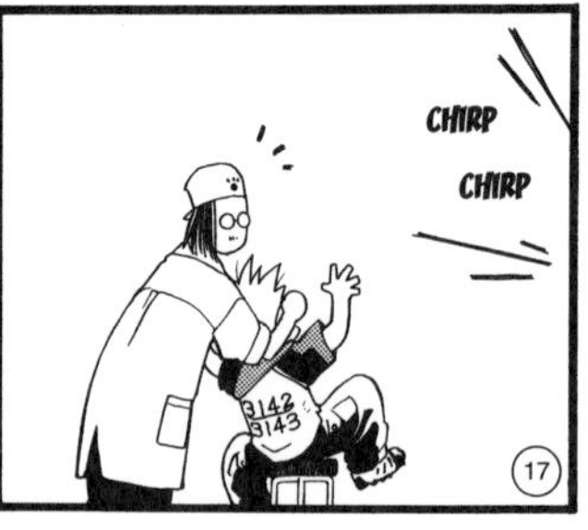
CHIRP
CHIRP

YES, MAY I HELP YOU?
チュンチュン
CHIRP
CHIRP
YOU, SEE, MY DAD'S GOT THIS ABILITY TO TALK TO ANIMALS.
2/3

どうぶつのみなさまへ
なんでもごそうだんください。
やしろどうぶつびょういん
Sorry. Japanese only!
HE RUNS AN ANIMAL CLINIC THAT ALSO OFFERS ANIMAL COUNSELING.
BUT!
AS YOU CAN SEE FROM THE LOOK OF THIS PLACE, HE'S NOT DOING TOO GOOD.
SURE HE'S HELPING OUT ANIMALS WITH THEIR PROBLEMS, BUT BEING NICE AND ALL AIN'T GONNA CUT IT IN THIS WORLD.
I DON'T EVER WANNA UNDERSTAND ANIMAL TALK AS LONG AS I LIVE.
BECAUSE IF I DID...
...LIFE'D BE EVEN MORE COMPLICATED.

HUMAN BEINGS ARE MUCH BETTER...
GOOD AFTERNOON.
GOOD AFTERNOON. HOW MAY I HELP YOU?
WELL...
...I'D LIKE TO HAVE MY DOG VACCINATED.
I SEE. PLEASE, RIGHT THIS WAY.

IS THIS YOUR FIRST VISIT?
YES.
THEN WILL YOU FILL OUT THIS FORM FOR ME?
SURE.
WOW!
WHAT A CUTIE!

STARE
ボー

HUH?
TWITCH

YOU'RE COVERED WITH SCRATCHES...
ARE YOU ALL RIGHT?

OH, MAN...
...WHAT DO I DO?

HMM...

I THINK YOU HAVE A FEVER, TOO.
ぴた
FUNAKOSHI WATA-SAN.
ぎゃふん

HERE!
LET'S GO, WATA.

TAKE CARE.
?

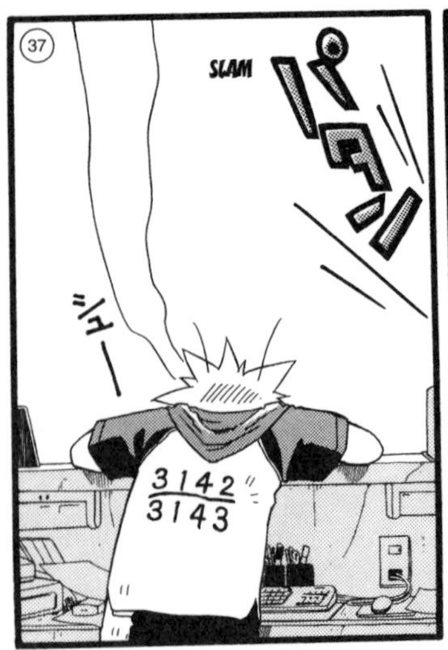
SLAM
パタン
3142
3143

ぎくしゃく
HEY, DAD, LEMME GIVE YOU A HAND.
OH, WHAT A PLEASANT SURPRISE. THANK YOU.

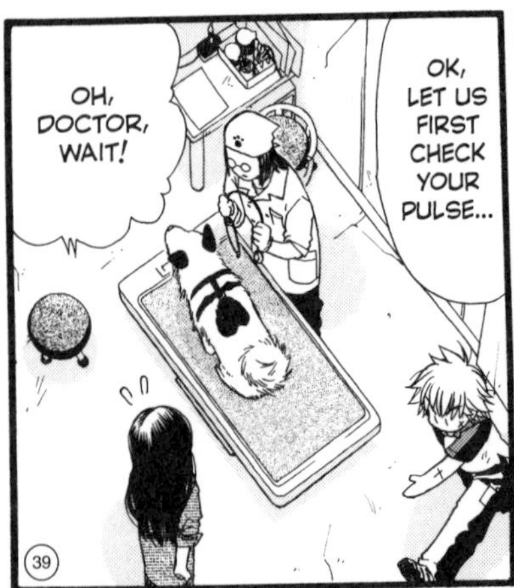
OK, LET US FIRST CHECK YOUR PULSE...
OH, DOCTOR, WAIT!

THERE.

SO HE'S A BITER, EH?

SO ADORABLE!

YOU THINK SO, TOO?
ESPECIALLY HIS DROOPY EAR...

OH, HE'S TALKING ABOUT THE DOG...
ANYBODY, HERE?
OH, GRANDMA SHIZU IS HERE.

TASUKE, PLEASE FILE THIS CARD.

47
OWNER'S NAME: FUNAKOSHI MISATO
飼主名 舟越みさと
PET'S NAME:
WATA
わー太
48
FUNAKOSHI MISATO...
SPARKLE
SPARKLE
SEE? HUMAN BEINGS ARE MUCH BETTER!
49
50
GOOD MORNING.
YOU COME HERE?
FUNAKOSHI MISATO !?
51
HOW DO YOU KNOW MY NAME?
HUH ?
THAT UNIFORM...
52
ARE YOU NEW HERE?
YES, I TRANSFERRED HERE TWO WEEKS AGO. I'M IN 3RD YEAR, CLASS A.
YOU'RE A 3RD YEAR!?
53
SHE'S A YEAR OLDER, EH?
I'M YASHIRO TASUKE. I'M IN 2ND YEAR, CLASS C.

HOW'S WATA-KUN? GUESS THAT'S A STUPID QUESTION SINCE I JUST SAW HIM YESTERDAY...
ははは
HA HA HA.
54
SNIFFLE
じわ
55
HUH ?
WHAT ?
STARE
じろ
STARE
じろ
56
うわア
UAH!
DID I SAY SOMETHING WRONG? I'M SOOO SORRY!
WHAT'S GOING ON?
57
402
I'M SORRY FOR CRYING ALL OF A SUDDEN.
ガチャ
58
THANKS FOR WALKING ME HOME...
わん
RUFF!
DON'T WORRY ABOUT IT.
59
ANYWAY, I DON'T THINK DOGS ARE ALLOWED IN APARTMENT COMPLEXES...
I KNOW ...
I'VE BEEN HIDING HIM...BUT THEY FOUND OUT...
60

WHY DON'T YOU FIND SOMEONE WHO'LL TAKE HIM.

I'VE BEEN TRYING, BUT I HAVEN'T BEEN ABLE TO FIND ANYONE.

OH NO!

61

STOP, WATA!

ガウ

ガウ

ガウ

62

しん…
SILENCE
63

HE DOESN'T LIKE BEING TOUCHED BY ANYONE OTHER THAN ME.
HE EVEN BITES MY PARENTS!
WHO'D WANT TO ADOPT THIS CRAZY MUTT!?
64

I'VE TRIED ALL SORTS OF WAYS TO STOP HIM FROM BITING, BUT THEY HAVEN'T WORKED.
ON TOP OF THAT, WATA ONLY KNOWS HOW TO SHAKE HANDS.
65

SIGH
66
IF ONLY I COULD TALK TO WATA...
HUH?
どき
67

DON'T YOU THINK SO?
DON'T YOU THINK IT'D BE GREAT IF PEOPLE CAN TALK TO THEIR PETS?
IF I COULD ONLY TALK TO WATA, THEN I'M SURE HE'D STOP BITING.
......
IF WATA DOESN'T STOP BITING...
...HE'LL BE...
MY DADDY SAID THAT HE'D TAKE WATA AWAY FROM ME!
HERE WE GO AGAIN!
C'MON, CHEER UP, MISATO-SENPAI!
I'LL HELP YOU FIND A NEW HOME FOR WATA!
REALLY?
YOU'RE THE BEST! THANK YOU SOOOO MUCH, TASUKE-KUN!
GRAB
SHE'S TOUCHING MY HAND...
AND SHE EVEN REMEMBERED MY NAME ♥
GIVE THIS DOG A HOME
NAME: WATA, 13 YEARS OLD, MALE, MIXED BREED
HE CAN SHAKE HANDS.
NOTE: HE BITES BUT IS A GOOD DOG.

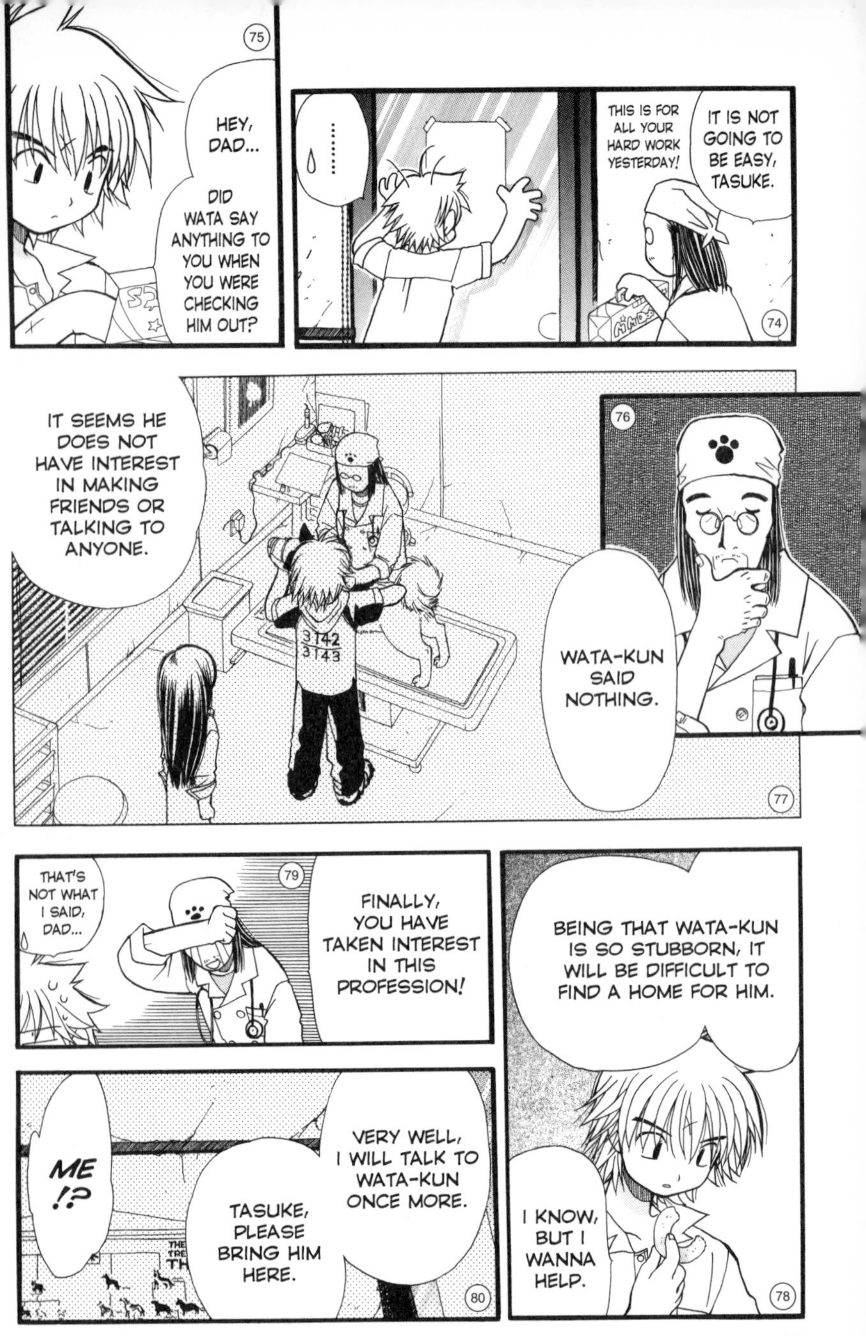

IT IS NOT GOING TO BE EASY, TASUKE.
THIS IS FOR ALL YOUR HARD WORK YESTERDAY!
......

HEY, DAD...
DID WATA SAY ANYTHING TO YOU WHEN YOU WERE CHECKING HIM OUT?

WATA-KUN SAID NOTHING.
IT SEEMS HE DOES NOT HAVE INTEREST IN MAKING FRIENDS OR TALKING TO ANYONE.

BEING THAT WATA-KUN IS SO STUBBORN, IT WILL BE DIFFICULT TO FIND A HOME FOR HIM.

I KNOW, BUT I WANNA HELP.

FINALLY, YOU HAVE TAKEN INTEREST IN THIS PROFESSION!

THAT'S NOT WHAT I SAID, DAD...

VERY WELL, I WILL TALK TO WATA-KUN ONCE MORE.

TASUKE, PLEASE BRING HIM HERE.

ME!?

81
ALL RIGHT, I'LL GO.
OH WELL. AT LEAST I GET TO TALK TO MISATO-SENPAI...
HEY, DAD...
82
...WHAT HAPPENS TO A PET IF THEIR OWNER CAN'T TAKE CARE OF 'EM?
WELL, IF THAT IS THE CASE...
83
...THE PET WOULD HAVE TO BE PUT TO SLEEP...
...OR...
84
...BE TAKEN TO THE POUND...
85
......
WONDER IF WATA KNOWS ABOUT THIS?

DOUBLE ELIZABETHAN COLLARS
ORIGINALLY, THIS WAS TO KEEP ANIMALS FROM LICKING THEIR WOUNDS, BUT CAN BE USED TO KEEP ANIMALS FROM BITING.
THE MUZZLE MISATO PUT ON IN ADVANCE
A LEASH
BITING-DOG COUNTERMEASURE
86
REALLY?
YEAH, I MIGHT'VE FOUND SOMEONE WHO'S INTERESTED IN ADOPTING HIM.
HOPE DAD'LL BE ABLE TO FIGURE HIM OUT...
WELL...
87
GLOVES FOR X-RAYS.
A PROTECTIVE X-RAY SUIT FOR ADDED PROTECTION.
88
PLEASE HOLD STILL FOR A MOMENT.
I AM GOING TO TAKE THIS MUZZLE OFF.
DAD, I DON'T THINK THAT'S A GOOD IDEA!
89
TASUKE, KEEP BACK.
BY THE WAY, WATA-KUN.
YOU UNDERSTAND YOUR SITUATION, DO YOU NOT?
DO YOU NOT WANT US TO HELP YOU FIND A NEW HOME?
90

91
....

92
ANYBODY HOME!?
TASUKE, PLEASE KEEP AN EYE ON WATA-KUN FOR A MOMENT.

93
......

94
YOU UNDERSTAND WHAT DAD'S SAYING, DON'T YOU?
YOU BETTER SPEAK UP OR ELSE...

95

96
NOT TO ME... TO MY DAD. I DON'T SPEAK OR UNDERSTAND DOG TALK.

97

IT IS NOT THAT YOU **CANNOT** UNDERSTAND.

IT IS THAT YOU **DO NOT** TRY.

98

!?

ガターン
TAKE CARE!
AAARRGH!
ぽっ
IT IS MISATO-DONO ALONE.
ぽた
SHE IS MY MASTER!
AND NO ONE ELSE!
WHAT THE!?
IS THIS WATA'S VOICE!?
FINE! WHATEVER...
...BUT GET THE HELL OFF OF ME!
...!?

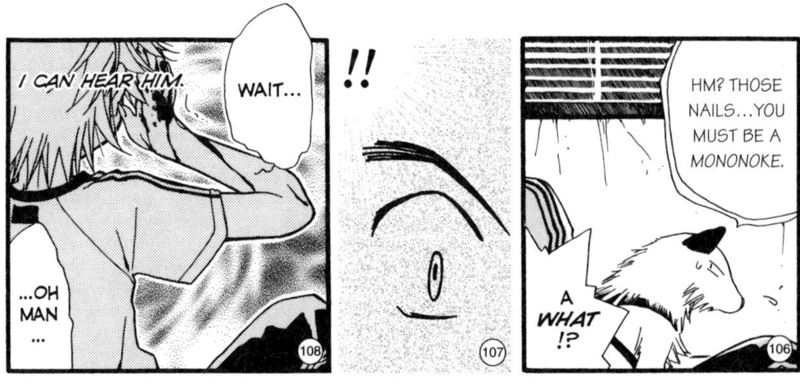
HM? THOSE NAILS…YOU MUST BE A MONONOKE.
A WHAT!?
106
!!
107
WAIT…
I CAN HEAR HIM.
…OH MAN…
108

109
I'M DREAMING, RIGHT? THIS IS ALL A NIGHTMARE, RIGHT!? HA HA HA!
IF YOU INSIST IT IS A DREAM, I CAN BITE YOUR OTHER HAND.

110
OH MAN, I CAN HEAR HIM CLEARLY.
IS SOMETHING THE MATTER, TASUKE?

111
ぱっ
CRAP!
BETTER NOT LET HIM SEE MY NAILS…

112
HM? ARE YOU HIDING SOMETHING FROM ME?
HUH? WHAT'RE YOU TALKIN' 'BOUT, DAD?

113
HA HA HA! STOP! THAT TICKLES!

114
がし
GRAB
HUH!
はっ

115

116
!?
(SIGH)
I ADVISE YOU TO NOT TRY AND TOUCH WATA-KUN AGAIN.

117
えーっと
NOW WHERE DID I PUT THE BAN-DAGES.
......

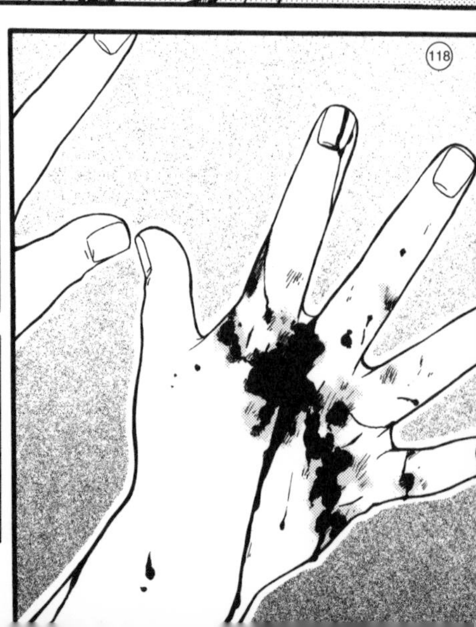
118

119
...THEY'RE BACK TO NORMAL...

120

HEY, YOU COULD SAY YOU'RE SORRY!
THAT BITE WAS WELL DESERVED, YOU MONONOKE!
ALL RIGHT, NO FIGHTING, YOU TWO!
TASUKE, THAT IS ENOUGH!
SHUT UP! LEMME GO!
THIS STUPID MUTT DOESN'T KNOW JACK!
HE'S GONNA BE LOCKED UP IN THE POUND...
I AM FULLY AWARE OF MY SITUATION.
... UNLESS...
SO WHAT, YOU WANNA DIE?
MISATO-DONO IS MY MASTER FOR LIFE.
NO ONE ELSE!
GOOD EVENING, IS ANYBODY HERE?
IT SOUNDS LIKE FUNAKOSHI MISATO-SAN IS HERE.

WATA!
YOU MUST TREAT YOUR SCAR, FIRST, TASUKE.
VETERINARIANS MUST NOT APPEAR BEFORE THEIR PATIENT'S OWNER BLEEDING LIKE THIS.
TASUKE.
WHAT!? I NEVER SAID I WAS GONNA BE A VET!
I SEE YOU HAVE FINALLY COME AROUND TO UNDER-STANDING ANIMALS.
WE WILL CELEBRATE LATER WITH A FEAST!
GREAT... NOW HE KNOWS.

RUFF!
RUFF!
I'M SORRY TO HAVE COME WITHOUT NOTICE. I WAS JUST SO WORRIED ABOUT WATA. BUT, UM...

...WHAT DID YOU THINK? DO YOU THINK HE'LL BE ABLE TO GET ALONG WELL WITH OTHERS?
YES, WELL ...

I KNEW IT... HE WON'T WILL HE?
?
WATA ...

HUF
HUF
...TASUKE-KUN.

TO THE BOTH OF YOU.
MY MASTER HAS COME, SO I AM LEAVING. GOODBYE.
WHAT THE HELL'S WRONG WITH YOU?
DON'T YOU WANNA LIVE!?
HAVE YOU EVER THOUGHT ABOUT MISATO-SENPAI'S FEELINGS?
YOU *IDIOT*!

145
TASUKE-KUN!?
I HAVE SPENT AGES WITH HUMAN BEINGS AND UNDERSTAND YOUR LANGUAGE AND YOUR WAY OF THINKING.
146
PERHAPS, A LITTLE TOO MUCH.
PERHAPS MISATO-DONO WILL UNDERSTAND...
147
!?
WATA-KUN!
148
149
WATA ...
150
タッ
FUNAKOSHI-SAN!
151
THAT STUPID MUTT!
TASUKE!
152
FUNAKOSHI-SAN, LET ME DRESS THAT BITE.
WATA ...
153
OH MY GOD... WHAT SHOULD I DO?
WATA HATES ME...

FUNA-KOSHI-SAN...
WHAT SHOULD I DO?
WATA...
THAT'S RIGHT.
I DIDN'T EVER WANNA UNDERSTAND ANIMAL TALK...
...BECAUSE IF I DID, LIFE'D BE MORE COMPLICATED...
...BECAUSE...
GRAB!
I WOULDN'T BE ABLE TO IGNORE THEM!
YOU OUTTA YOUR MIND!?
WHY THE HELL D'YOU BITE MISATO-SENPAI!?

C'MON, WE'RE GOING BACK. YOU GOTTA SAY YOU'RE SORRY OR SHE'LL *REALLY* HATE YOU!
THAT IS MY INTENTION.
161

WHAT D'YOU SAY?
162

NOW …
…I HAVE NO REGRETS.
163

164

TASUKE, WAS IT?
WILL YOU PLEASE TAKE ME TO THE POUND?
165

………
I BEG YOU, PLEASE.
166

C'MON, WE'RE GOING HOME!
ズル
YANK!
TASUKE, WHAT ARE YOU…
167

THIS IS WHY I DIDN'T WANNA UNDERSTAND YOU ANIMALS!
168

UM, DOCTOR...
YES?
I'VE... NEVER BEEN BIT BY A DOG BEFORE...
I SEE...IT HURTS, DOES IT NOT? IT WILL SWELL LATER ON...
IT *REALLY* HURTS...
I KNOW.
BUT YOU MUST UNDERSTAND THAT WATA-KUN IS IN PAIN, TOO.
MISATO-SENPAI !!
TASUKE-KUN ...
... WATA.

WATA!

I'M SOO SORRY, WATA!
I SHOULD'VE THOUGHT MORE ABOUT HOW *YOU* FEEL!
NO WONDER YOU HATE ME...
BUT WATA...

...I LOVE YOU SO MUCH!
I DON'T WANT YOU TO DIE!

PLEASE LET ME HELP YOU!
PLEASE DON'T DIE!
!!
MISATO-SENPAI...

...*I'LL* TAKE CARE OF WATA.

(182)
WHAT!?
REALLY, TASUKE-KUN?
AS A MATTER OF FACT, I HAVE A REQUEST FOR WATA-KUN.

(183)
DAD?
I HAVE BEEN LOOKING FOR A GOOD BLOOD DONOR DOG.
HE IS A LITTLE OLD, BUT HE HAS GOOD LINES.

(184)
WON'T YOU HELP US,...
...WATA-KUN?

(185)

(186)
REALLY, DOCTOR?
REALLY!?

(187)
TH-THEN CAN I COME AND VISIT WATA FROM TIME TO TIME?
BY ALL MEANS.
ぱん

188
HEY, WATA. SO NOW YOU KNOW HOW MISATO-SENPAI FEELS.
SHE STILL LOVES YOU EVEN THOUGH YOU BIT HER. C'MON, WATA, LISTEN TO HER.

189

VERY WELL.
190

ABOUT BEFORE ...
191
HUH?
WHEN I CAME INTO THE CLINIC TO SEE WATA...

192
IT LOOKED LIKE YOU WERE TALKING TO HIM...
REALLY? WAS I TALKIN' TO HIM?

193
YEAH, BUT ANYWAY, ARE YOU GONNA BE A VET LIKE YOUR DAD?
WELL, UH...

194
I KNEW IT!!
I WANNA BE A VET ONE DAY, TOO!

195
GOOD LUCK TO THE BOTH OF US!
ぎゅ
SQUEEZE
Y-YES! GOOD LUCK TO US BOTH!

196
SEE YOU, WATA! GOOD NIGHT!
I'LL COME SEE YOU AGAIN TOMOR-ROW!
わん
RUFF!

197
TASUKE.

TWITCH
IT SEEMS YOU HAVE ADOPTED ME INTO YOUR FAMILY TO GET CLOSER TO MISATO-DONO...
198
IF YOU DARE LAY EVEN ONE FINGER ON MY MASTER...
MY SHARP FANGS WILL PIERCE THROUGH YOUR NECK!
NYAH, NYAH! YOU CAN'T STOP ME!
199
ARE YOU GONNA BE A VET LIKE YOUR DAD?
WELL, UH...
200
GOOD LUCK TO THE BOTH OF US!
Y-YES!
201
GOOD LUCK TO THE BOTH OF US, TASUKE-KUN!
GIMME BACK THAT TAPE!
I'M NOT GONNA BE A VET!
202

CHAPTER 2: MAEKAWA SALLY (PART 1)

TASUKE-KUN, IT WAS LIKE LOVE AT FIRST SIGHT...
WILL YOU GO OUT WITH ME?
はは
HA HA! OF COURSE!
NOW COME TO ME, MY SWEET MISATO!
ぎゅ
TASUKE-KUN!
MISATO!!
HUH?
ぎゅう
HEY, THAT KINDA HURTS...
HEY, CUT THAT OUT...
OUCH!

9
OW OW OW OW OW OW!
10
ガタッ
ドカ
バタ
ドカッドカ

ポカポカ
GOOD MORNING, TASUKE, WATA-KUN.
ぽく
LEMME GO, YOU STUPID MUTT!
WHY THE HELL D'YOU BITE ME, ANYWAY?
YOU HAD A VERY STRANGE LOOK ON YOUR FACE...
I AM GUESSING YOU WERE HAVING QUITE A DREAM... PERHAPS ONE THAT IS VULGAR.
WH...
...WHAT'RE YOU TALKING ABOUT!?
AND STOP LOOKIN' AT ME LIKE THAT, DAD!

IT'S STILL EARLY!
ふぁ
(YAWN) I'M GOIN' BACK TO BED.
OH, TASUKE.
ARE YOU NOT FORGETTING ABOUT SOMETHING?
ぽん

HUH? WHAT'RE THESE FOR?

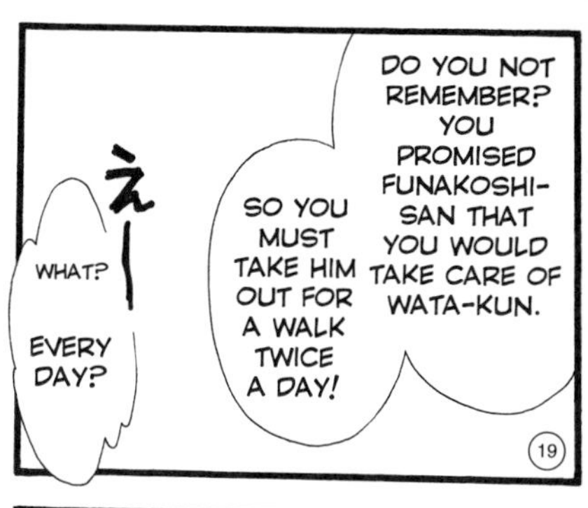
DO YOU NOT REMEMBER? YOU PROMISED FUNAKOSHI-SAN THAT YOU WOULD TAKE CARE OF WATA-KUN.
SO YOU MUST TAKE HIM OUT FOR A WALK TWICE A DAY!
えー
WHAT? EVERY DAY?

WHAT IF IT'S POURIN' RAIN?
EVERYDAY NO MATTER WHAT. HOW WOULD YOU FEEL IF YOU COULD NOT GO TO THE RESTROOM? THAT UNPLEASANT FEELING IS MUTUAL TO HUMANS AND ANIMALS.

WHAT A PAIN IN THE BUTT...

W-WELL, I'VE GOTTA GET READY FOR SCHOOL. YOU'VE GOT NOTHIN' TO DO. WHY DON'T *YOU* TAKE HIM?

I DO NOT MIND WALKING MYSELF.

NO, NO, WATA-KUN. YOU SHOULD NOT GO OUTSIDE ALONE!

TASUKE, WATA-KUN IS WAITING!

(YAWN) BACK TO BED...

HUH?

24

OH, THAT?

IT IS AN APPLICATION TO THE ASHIBU UNIVERSITY VETERINARY MEDICINE DEPARTMENT... YOU CAN COMMUTE FROM HERE AND IT WILL NOT BE SO EXPENSIVE.

25

第2学年 進路希望調

2年 C組 番号 21

氏名 社 太助

1. 大学(4年生·短大·その

第一: ~~大日本経済大学~~ 葦布大学 獣医学部

第二: ~~大和大学~~ 東日本畜産大学獣医学部

I WANT YOU TO BECOME A GREAT ANIMAL COUNSELOR!

26

HOP

27

WHAT THE HELL'S YOUR PROBLEM, DAD? IT'S *MY* FUTURE! YOU DON'T HAVE TO DO *ANYTHING* FOR ME. GOT IT?

OH, COME NOW, TASUKE. THERE IS NO REASON TO OVER-REACT.

PLUS, ANIMAL COUNSEL-ING IS A VERY FULFILLING OCCUPA-TION.

28
ピク
TWITCH
FULFILLING !?
29
ボロッ
YOU CALL *THIS* BEING FULFILLED?
'N' JUST CUZ I UNDERSTAND ANIMAL TALK DOESN'T MEAN I'M GONNA BE AN ANIMAL COUNSELOR!

I'M GONNA GET A *REAL* JOB AND MAKE LOTS OF MONEY!

I'M NOT GONNA SETTLE FOR FAST FOOD! I'M GONNA BE EATIN' SUSHI, BLOWFISH, EEL AND ALL THAT EXPENSIVE STUFF!

HUF, HUF

OH, AND SUKIYAKI, TOO.

する…

I CANNOT BELIEVE WHAT I AM HEARING.

DID YOU HEAR THAT, DEAR?

DO YOU NOT THINK IT IS THE PERFECT OCCUPATION FOR OUR SON?

WHAT DO YOU THINK, DEAR?
HE CAN ONLY TALK TO WATA-KUN NOW, BUT HE HAS A BRIGHT FUTURE AHEAD OF HIM AS AN ANIMAL COUNSELOR.
RIGHT NOW HE ONLY HAS THE CLAWS, BUT SOON HE WILL HAVE EARS AND A TAIL, WILL HE NOT, DEAR?
HUH!

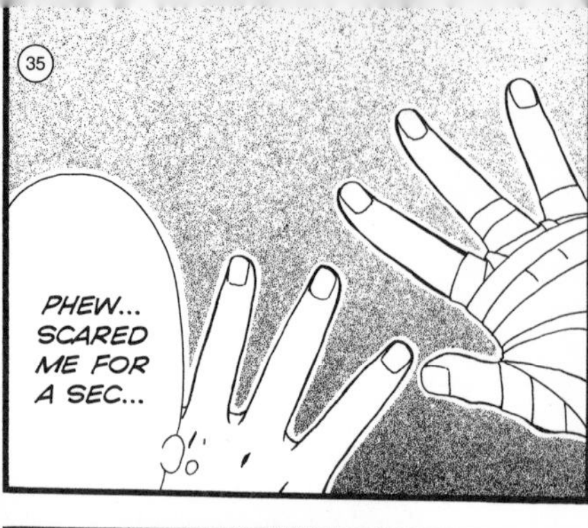
PHEW... SCARED ME FOR A SEC...

BUT HOW DOES HE KNOW ABOUT THE CLAWS?
WATA-KUN TOLD ME.
HE MUST'VE BEEN SEEIN' THINGS. I DON'T GOT CLAWS.
ワンワン
YOU MIGHT HAVE 'EM, BUT *I'M* NOT LIKE YOU, DAD.

ガチャ
GOOD MORNING!
I'M HERE TO SEE WATA! CAN I TAKE HIM OUT FOR A WALK?

AH, TASUKE-KUN, GOOD MORNING.
MISATO!!
あっ
OOPS!
I MEAN...
と
SENPAI!

FLOAT

I KNEW IT!

ARE YOU THINKING OF GOING TO ASHIBU UNIVERSITY, TASUKE-KUN?
EH?
YOU, TOO, SENPAI?

I'VE ALREADY APPLIED! GOOD LUCK TO THE BOTH OF US!
SQUEEZE
OH!
YEAH, GOOD LUCK TO US BOTH!

WELL, I'M GONNA TAKE WATA FOR HIS WALK!
RUFF!
ALL RIGHT ...
... TAKE CARE ...

NO, WAIT UP, MISATO-SENPAI! I'LL COME WITH YOU!

HEY. MISATO-SENPAI...

...IF YOU WANT, I CAN WALK WATA UNTIL YOUR EXAMS ARE OVER.
NO, IT'S OK.
JUST SITTING DOWN AND STUDYING ALL THE TIME'S NOT GOOD FOR YOU. THESE WALKS GIVE ME A CHANCE TO TAKE A BREAK.

PLUS, I WANT TO DO IT.
I WANT TO SPEND AS MUCH TIME WITH WATA AS POSSIBLE.
HUH? WHY?

WHY? WOULDN'T YOU WANT TO SPEND AS MUCH TIME WITH SOMEONE YOU LIKE?
YES, I WOULD!
ズイ

ズイ

STAY OUTTA MY WAY!
わし
わし
もが
YOU FIEND! YOU MUST BE PLANNING SOMETHING EVIL!
I MUST PROTECT MISATO-DONO FROM THE LIKES OF YOU!

DO I LOOK LIKE I'D HURT MISATO-SENPAI!
I'M NO MONSTER!
BUT YOU ARE A MONONOKE!

I DIDN'T THINK YOU AND WATA WERE SUCH GOOD FRIENDS, TASUKE-KUN!

(56)

OH!

(57)

(58)

(59)

WOW ♥

AN IRISH SETTER. HOW CUTE!

BUT SHE'S SO SKINNY...

(60)

....

WHY SO SKINNY?

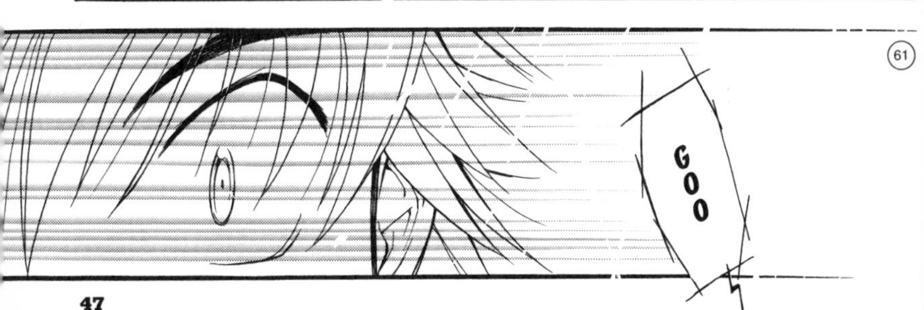

HUH?
THOUGHT I HEARD A VOICE...
MUST'VE BEEN THE SETTER'S STOMACH GROWLING...
は
YEAH, THAT'S IT!
I DIDN'T HEAR ANY VOICES! HA HA HA!
NO WAY!
?
SALLY, NO!

69
TASUKE-KUN, LOOK OUT!
70
HUH?
71
WAAAAUH!
72

WATA!
ビク
TWITCH
BAD GIRL!
オロオロ
I'M TERRIBLY SORRY, YOUNG MAN! ARE YOU OK?
....

WHAT THE!?

DID WATA JUST PROTECT ME?

WATA, ARE YOU OK?
HUH!
I'M REALLY SORRY.
SHE JUST HAD PUPPIES LAST WEEK AND THE SIGHT OF ANOTHER DOG SEEMS TO SET HER OFF.

I BELIEVE THERE IS AN ANIMAL CLINIC AROUND HERE. LET US GO THERE IMMEDIATELY.
MY DAD RUNS THAT CLINIC!
AND I'M FINE. NOTHING TO WORRY ABOUT, MISS.

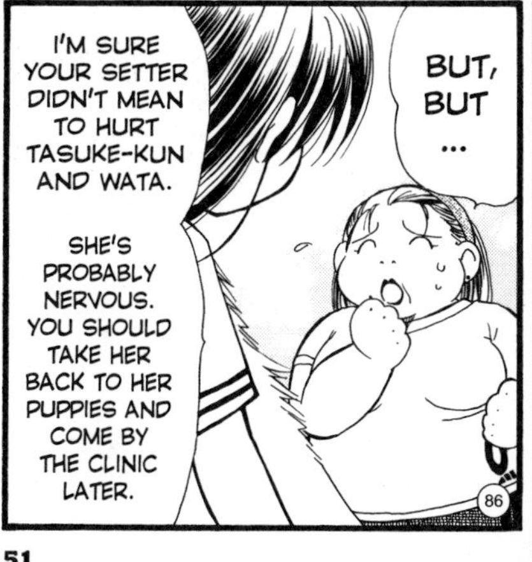
BUT, BUT ...
I'M SURE YOUR SETTER DIDN'T MEAN TO HURT TASUKE-KUN AND WATA.
SHE'S PROBABLY NERVOUS. YOU SHOULD TAKE HER BACK TO HER PUPPIES AND COME BY THE CLINIC LATER.

OK, I'LL DO THAT.
I REALLY AM SORRY!

WATA, ARE YOU OK?
THIS SHOULD STOP THE BLEED-ING.
ぎゅ
SQUEEZE

TASUKE-KUN, LET'S GET WATA BACK TO YOUR DAD'S CLINIC.
CLASSES ARE GONNA START SOON. YOU SHOULD GET GOING TO SCHOOL, SENPAI. I'LL TAKE WATA BACK TO THE CLINIC.

WAIT, I'M COMING WITH YOU!
がし
YOU'VE GOT EXAMS TO TAKE. PLUS, IT'LL TAKE LONGER IF THE BOTH OF US GO. DON'T WORRY, SENPAI, I'LL TAKE HIM.
I'LL TELL YOU HOW WATA'S DOIN' LATER, OK?

SEE YA LATER!
TASUKE-KUN...

WATA...

94

THANK YOU SO MUCH, TASUKE-KUN!

95

96

HEY, WATA.

HOW'RE YOU DOING?

97

HEY, ABOUT BEFORE... YOU KNOW, PROTECTING ME AND ALL...

UM...

98

...THANKS.

99

100
YOU HAVE IT ALL WRONG, YOUNG BOY!
101
I DID NOT PROTECT **YOU!**
I WAS PROTECTING THAT **SETTER!**
102
103
WHAT?
104
FOR DOGS SUCH AS US, HURTING HUMANS IS A QUICK ROAD TO DEATH.
THAT SETTER HAS HER CHILDREN ...
SHE SHOULD NOT FORSAKE HER NEWBORN CHILDREN FOR SOMETHING LIKE THIS.
105
WATA ...

106
EXCUSE ME.
?
HEY, WHERE'RE YOU GOING? THE CLINIC'S THE OTHER WAY!

107
I AM GOING TO LOOK IN ON THE LADY.
HUH?

108
YOU CRAZY? DON'T YOU REMEMBER WHAT THAT SETTER DID TO YOU?
IF YOU GET HURT ANY MORE, MISATO-SENPAI'LL *REALLY* HATE ME!
...TASUKE.

109
DID YOU NOT SEE THE LADY'S TEARS?
TEARS!?

THERE MUST BE A REASON SHE ACTED THE WAY SHE DID.
AS A MAN, I CANNOT IGNORE A BEAUTIFUL LADY IN TIMES OF TROUBLE AND GRIEF.
110

ひょこ
ひら
HEY, WHAT ABOUT YOUR LEG?
とぼ
SIGH
WHY DO YOU GOTTA BE ALL CHIVAL-ROUS?
......
SIGH
HEY, WATA, WAIT UP!
I'LL GO WITH YOU!

GAUGAU WATA
BOW WOW WATA
TM

CHAPTER 3: MAEKAWA SALLY (PART 2)

2
YOU MUST BE FROM THE ANIMAL COUNSELING CENTER I'VE HEARD SO MUCH ABOUT.
DOG
DOG
MAEKAWA
3
SALLY
I AM TERRIBLY SORRY FOR BITING YOU. MY NAME IS MAEKAWA SALLY.
よろ
キュー
キュー
HOW IS YOUR LEG DOING?
4
...
MY LEG IS FINE. THERE IS NOTHING TO WORRY ABOUT.
5
WHAT THE HELL AM I DOING? I COULD BE ARRESTED FOR THIS...

SALLY-DONO, YOU APPEARED TO BE RATHER UPSET ABOUT SOME-THING...
IF YOU DO NOT MIND...
...PLEASE TELL US WHAT IT IS THAT CAUSES YOU GRIEF.
YES... WELL...

MY GOD! IS THIS TRUE?

IS WHAT TRUE?
I SEE. SO THAT IS WHY YOU ARE SO DISTRESSED ...

SALLY-DONO IS ASKING FOR YOUR HELP IN THIS MATTER.
I SHALL INTERPRET WHAT SHE SAYS, SO LISTEN CAREFULLY.
UNLIKE YOU *DOGS*, I'VE GOT SCHOOL TO GO TO...

I'M LISTEN-ING...

WELL ...
がさ
RUSTLE
... ONE OF MY CHILDREN IS MISSING.
MISSING ?

IN MY FAMILY, THE NUMBER OF CHILDREN WE BEAR ALWAYS EQUALS THE NUMBER OF ... WE HAVE.
MY MOTHER, GRANDMOTHER, GREAT-GRAND-MOTHER— IT HAS ALWAYS BEEN THE SAME.

...? EQUAL TO WHAT ?
ごにょごにょ
SHE SAID ...
HUH?
CAN'T HEAR YOU.

NIPPLES.
OH... SORRY.

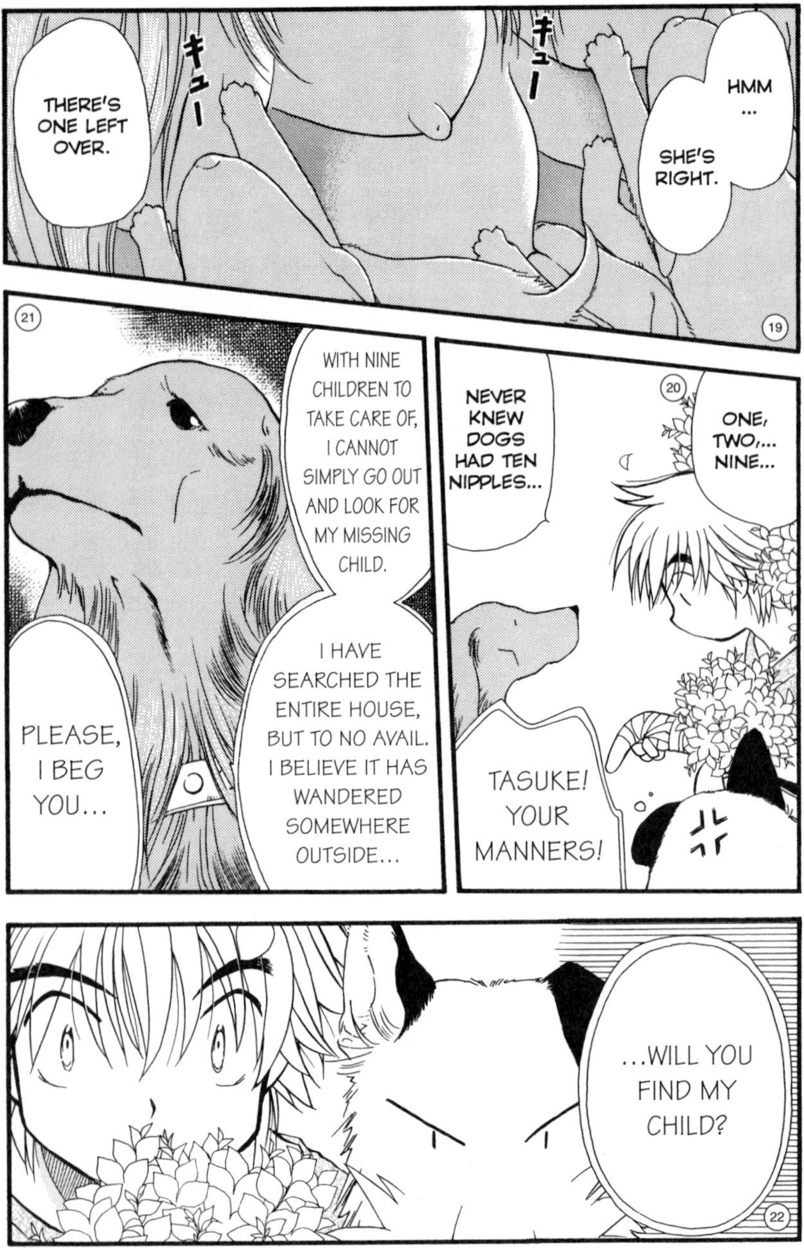

HMM ...
SHE'S RIGHT.
キュー
キュー
THERE'S ONE LEFT OVER.
(19)

(20)
ONE, TWO,... NINE...
NEVER KNEW DOGS HAD TEN NIPPLES...
TASUKE! YOUR MANNERS!

(21)
WITH NINE CHILDREN TO TAKE CARE OF, I CANNOT SIMPLY GO OUT AND LOOK FOR MY MISSING CHILD.
I HAVE SEARCHED THE ENTIRE HOUSE, BUT TO NO AVAIL. I BELIEVE IT HAS WANDERED SOMEWHERE OUTSIDE...
PLEASE, I BEG YOU...

...WILL YOU FIND MY CHILD?
(22)

IT AIN'T GONNA BE EASY, WATA...
CS バッテリー
ANYWAY, I'M SURE IT'LL FIND ITS WAY BACK HOME.
WE SHOULD GO BACK TO THE CLINIC AND TAKE CARE OF YOUR LEG INSTEAD.
YANK!
YANK!
MY LEG IS FINE!
AND SALLY-DONO SAID SHE IS CERTAIN HER CHILD IS OUTSIDE HER HOME.
OUT-SIDE, HUH?
ARE YOU SURE YOU HAD TEN PUPPIES? MAYBE YOU HAD NINE?
NO!
I AM CERTAIN! I HAVE ***TEN*** NIPPLES AND ***TEN*** CHIL-DREN.
IT BREAKS MY HEART JUST THINKING ABOUT MY CHILD BEING OUT THERE ALL ALONE...
キュー
キュー

DO NOT FRET, SALLY-DONO! WE SHALL FIND YOUR CHILD!
REALLY?
GROWL
MAN, I'M STARVING!
HMM... MAYBE I'LL EAT BEFORE I GO TO SCHOOL...
I'M ALREADY LATE FOR FIRST PERIOD ANYWAY...
TASUKE! HOW CAN YOU BE SO SELFISH? LET US FIND THE CHILD *FIRST!*
LOOK. I BET SALLY COUNTED WRONG.
SHE PROBABLY ONLY HAD *NINE* PUPPIES.
WE'RE JUST WASTING OUR TIME!
WHY DON'T WE JUST TELL HER WE COULDN'T FIND IT?
I AM EXTREMELY DISAP-POINTED IN YOU.
CLANG, CLANG

WHY ARE YOU GIVING UP BEFORE WE START!? HOW CAN YOU JUMP SO QUICKLY TO SUCH CONCLUSIONS?
HEY, IT'S JUST A WEEK-OLD PUPPY!
IT CAN'T EVEN SEE YET!
BUT WE MUST LOOK FOR THE CHILD UNTIL SALLY-DONO IS SATISFIED.
EVEN IF...
... YOU **ARE** RIGHT.
WATA ... YOU...
SO YOU DON'T THINK THERE'S A TENTH PUPPY EITHER, DO YOU?
THEN WHY LOOK AND WASTE OUR TIME?
IT IS NOT A WASTE OF TIME.
IF WE DO NOT DO SOMETHING, SALLY-DONO WILL GROW FEEBLE—PUTTING HER OTHER NINE CHILDREN AT RISK.

BY TAKING OUR TIME TO LOOK FOR THE CHILD, WE WILL SATISFY EVERYBODY.

FINE, WE'LL LOOK UNTIL YOUR SATISFIED.
TASUKE !

DON'T GET ME WRONG. I'M JUST KEEPIN' THE PROMISE I MADE WITH MISATO-SENPAI.
IF I LET YOU WALK ON YOUR OWN, SHE'D HATE ME!
I'M JUST GONNA HOLD YOUR LEASH SO DO WHATEVER YOU WANNA DO.
SHH!
EXCELLENT !

HEY, HE'S TALKING TO HIMSELF.

I'M BEAT! FOOD! FOOD!
STOP WHINING! IT HAS ONLY BEEN ONE DAY!

!!
YOU'RE NOT THINKING OF LOOKING TOMORROW, ARE YOU?
WATA !

WATA !
がばっ

MISATO-SENPAI !?

HUH!

OH ...

UH- OH...

YOU SAID YOU'D CALL AND LET ME KNOW HOW WATA WAS DOING! DO YOU KNOW HOW WORRIED I'VE BEEN?

ON TOP OF THAT, HIS LEG HASN'T EVEN BEEN TREATED!

UM... I'M SORRY. I FORGOT ...
"FORGOT" ?
HOW COULD YOU? YOU KNOW HOW MUCH I LOVE WATA...
AND YOU FORGOT ?
NO, DON'T CRY! I'M SOOOO SORRY !

THERE !
THIS SHOULD DO IT.
THANK YOU VERY MUCH, DOCTOR.
I'LL COME AGAIN TOMORROW.
OK. TAKE CARE.
ANIMAL HOSPITAL
やしろ動物

つーーん
PHEW! GOOD THING HIS LEG ISN'T THAT HURT!

ガーん

......

....
HA HA HA.

ぐにぐに

LET US GO INSIDE.
THE X-RAYS SHOULD BE READY BY NOW.
X-RAYS? WE HAVE A PATIENT?

!?
SALLY !!

MAEKAWA-SAN CAME TO APOLOGIZE THIS AFTERNOON.
THEN THIS EVENING, SHE BROUGHT SALLY-SAN HERE BECAUSE HER CONDITION TOOK A SUDDEN TURN FOR THE WORSE...
MAEKAWA-SAN HAS ALREADY GONE HOME TO PREPARE DINNER FOR HER FAMILY.
A SUDDEN TURN FOR THE WORSE!?

There is no need to worry.
She is a little under-nourished. She felt dizzy and could not stand up, but she's ok now.
63
Sally-dono!
Oh, Wata-sama. I am sorry to have troubled you.
But I'm fine now.
64

Oh? Was Wata-kun the one who was looking for your puppy?
Huh? Tasuke, too?
Oh ♥
Well, well ♥
65
Tasuke has finally decided to become an animal counselor ♪
I'm not gonna be an animal doc, Dad!
We must celebrate!
Doctor, what do you mean by Sally-dono being "ok"?
66

Oh, take a look...
... at this X-ray.
67

X-ray? Of Sally?
Yes.
Click
When she told me about her condition, I thought maybe, and checked her womb...
68

It is rare but sometimes happens. During delivery, the symptoms disappear and...
69
70
71

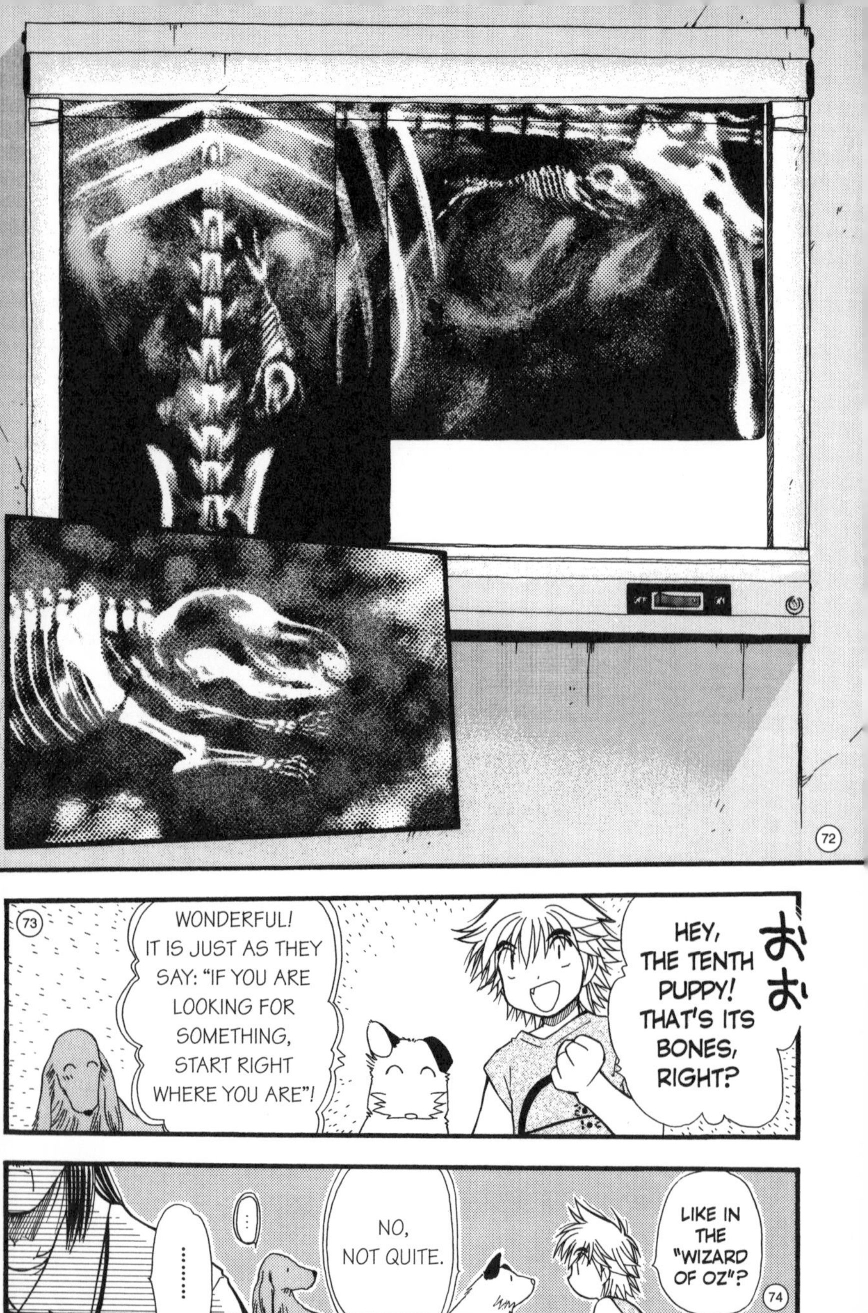

72

73
おお
HEY, THE TENTH PUPPY! THAT'S ITS BONES, RIGHT?
WONDERFUL! IT IS JUST AS THEY SAY: "IF YOU ARE LOOKING FOR SOMETHING, START RIGHT WHERE YOU ARE"!

LIKE IN THE "WIZARD OF OZ"?
74
NO, NOT QUITE.
...
....

75
ANYWAY, THERE REALLY WERE TEN PUPPIES!
THAT'S GREAT, SALLY!
YES!
Y...YES!
THANK YOU ALL SO VERY MUCH.

76
NO...
...IT IS ALREADY TOO LATE.

77
TOO LATE?
SALLY-SAN, PLEASE STAY CALM AND LISTEN CAREFULLY TO WHAT I HAVE TO SAY.

78

I'M AFRAID THE FETUS IS *ALREADY DEAD.*

WHAT?
HOW CAN YOU BE SO SURE!?
YOU CAN'T TELL IF IT'S DEAD OR ALIVE BY AN X-RAY!
YES, I CAN.
79
80

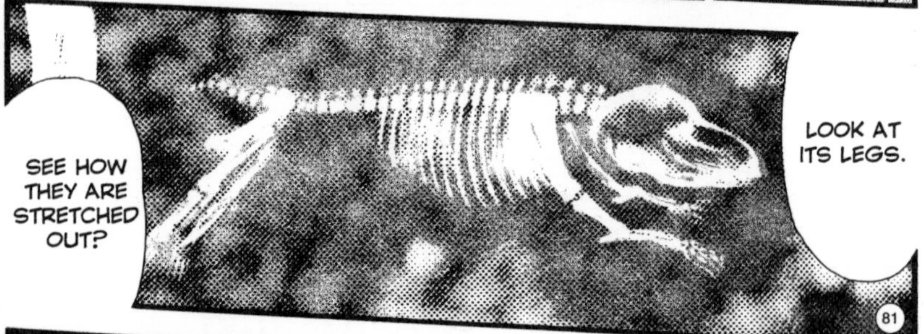
LOOK AT ITS LEGS.
SEE HOW THEY ARE STRETCHED OUT?
81

IF THE FETUS WERE ALIVE...
パラ
82

...ITS LEGS WOULD BE BENT.
83

N... NO.
MY CHILD... NO... I SHOULD HAVE REALIZED THAT IT WAS STILL IN MY WOMB...
84

SALLY-DONO, PLEASE...
... DO NOT BLAME YOURSELF.
I AM VERY SORRY, SALLY-SAN.
85

BAM!
86
87
TASUKE ...
じんじんじん
OW! FORGOT ABOUT MY HAND...
88
GOO...
89
GOO
90
GOO
91
WHAT IS THE MATTER, TASUKE ?
THAT SOUND ...

SOUND ?
I DID NOT HEAR ANYTHING.

WHAT?

BUT I'M SURE I HEARD...

NO!

IT'S NOT THE SOUND OF A GROWLING STOMACH I'VE BEEN HEARING...

DAD !

DAD, PLEASE!
GET THE PUPPY OUT RIGHT NOW!
TASUKE !?
IT'S NOT TOO LATE!
HURRY !!

98

99

グゥ

キュウ

100

I WOULD HAVE NEVER THOUGHT IT WAS A CASE OF SUSPENDED ANIMATION.

ジャー

IT TRULY IS A MIRACLE.

101

102

103
SEE?
DO YOU NOT THINK DOCTORS WITH OUR ABILITIES ARE A NECESSITY?
はっ
HUH!
104
I'M STILL NOT GONNA BE A VET, DAD!
I DON'T WANNA WASTE MY TIME WITH STUFF LIKE THIS.
すたすた
REALLY? BUT IT IS SO FULFILLING.
105
YOU HEARD THE PUPPY'S CRY. I DID NOT.
TASUKE ...
106
...YOUR ABILITY SAVED A LIFE TODAY.
107
....
108
NAH, MUST'VE BEEN A FLUKE...

CHAPTER 4:
WHAT IT TAKES TO BE A LEADER

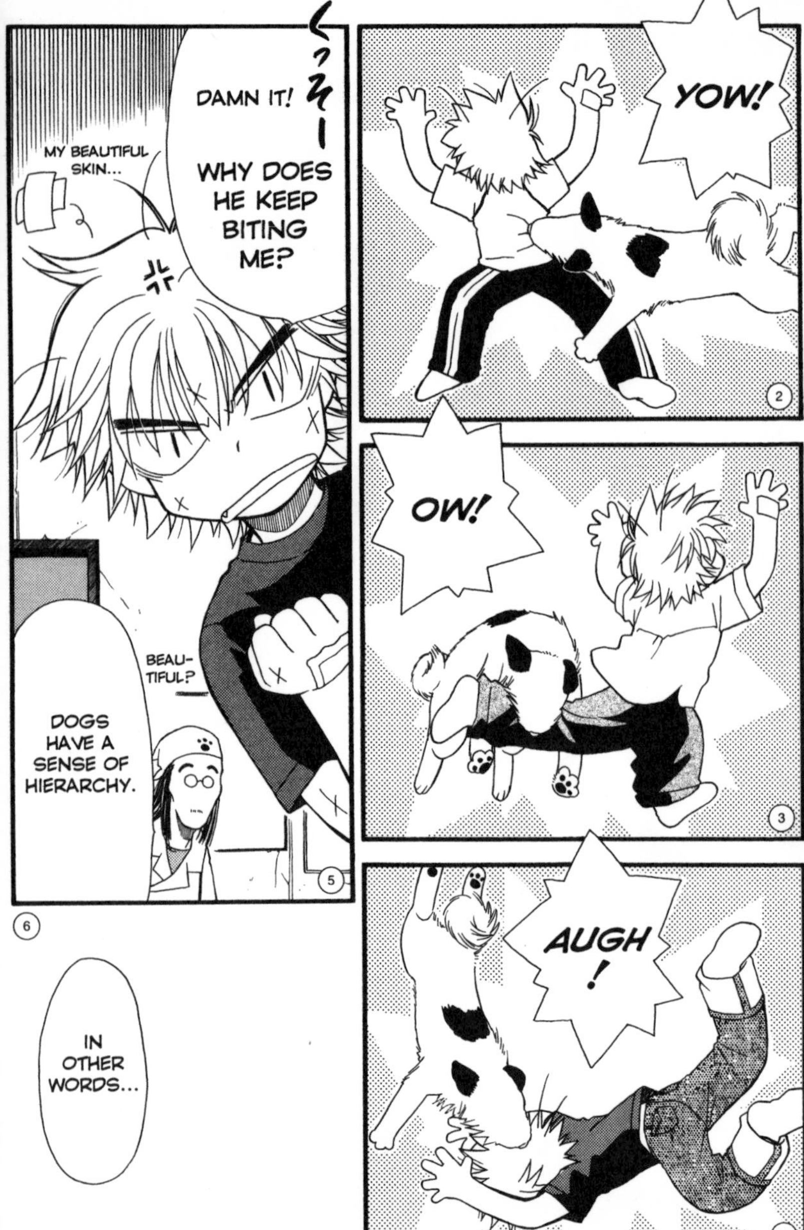
YOW!
OW!
AUGH!
DAMN IT!
くっそー
WHY DOES HE KEEP BITING ME?
MY BEAUTIFUL SKIN...
BEAU-TIFUL?
DOGS HAVE A SENSE OF HIERARCHY.
IN OTHER WORDS...

WATA-KUN'S SOCIAL STATUS IS ***HIGHER*** THAN YOURS.
ぴきき
SUPERIOR
WATA
INFERIOR
TASUKE

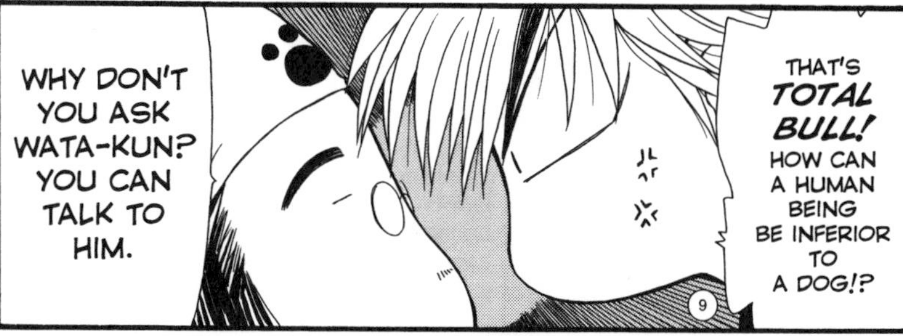
THAT'S ***TOTAL BULL!*** HOW CAN A HUMAN BEING BE INFERIOR TO A DOG!?
WHY DON'T YOU ASK WATA-KUN? YOU CAN TALK TO HIM.

うがー
ARRRGH! I'M HUMAN, DAMN IT! I DON'T WANNA TALK TO ANIMALS!!

AND EVEN IF I DID, I'D ***NEVER*** TALK AN OLD, ROTTEN, UNFRIENDLY MUTT LIKE WATA!

RUFF!
ワーン
RUFF!

THAT BARK BY WATA...

IT'S GOTTA BE MISATO-SENPAI!

LATER, DAD! I'M GOIN' FOR A WALK!
くる
HEY, MISATO-SENPAI ♪
HELLO, DR. YASHIRO. HOW ARE YOU DOING?
わん
RUFF!
AND HE SAYS HE DOESN'T WANT TO TALK TO ANIMALS ...
BUT TASUKE KNEW MISATO-SAN WAS HERE JUST BY HEARING WATA-KUN BARK.
RIGHT, DEAR ?
DOCTOR, ARE YOU IN?
ドー
YES.
MISATO-SENPAI!
スタスタ
つーん
MISA...
IS SHE STILL MAD THAT I DIDN'T TAKE CARE OF WATA'S LEG?
MAN, WHAT TO DO...

ムカ
COME TO THINK OF IT, IT'S NOT MY FAULT.
WATA WAS THE ONE WHO WANTED TO HELP SALLY!
ムカ

THAT DAMN DOG!

TASUKE-KUN, I GIVE UP.

HUH?
I'M TIRED OF BEING MAD.

YOU'RE THE ONLY ONE WHO GETS ALONG WITH WATA.
AND YOU CUT CLASS TO PLAY WITH WATA, RIGHT?
HUH?
UM...

... YEAH! YEAH, I DID!

ミるっ
WATA'S JUST SOOOO CUTE!
ESPECIALLY THIS BUSHY PART ON HIS CHEST!
KEEP YOUR PAWS OFF ME, FIEND!

RIGHT?
I'M SO GLAD YOU TWO GET ALONG SO WELL.
WATA, YOU'RE SO LUCKY THAT YOU MET TASUKE-KUN AND HIS FATHER.

あっはっは
HA HA HA!
WHY DON'T WE ALL HUG!
OH!
ガー
GRRR!

WELL, SEE YOU TOMORROW, TASUKE-KUN!

AND DON'T BE LATE TO SCHOOL, OK?
BE GOOD, WATA.
わん
RUFF!
GOOD NIGHT!

MISATO-SENPAI'S CUTE EVEN WHEN SHE'S ANGRY...
AH... "SEE YOU TOMORROW..."
IT'S LIKE WE'RE A COUPLE... HEH HEH.
SMIRK

ガブッ
BITE!

JUST LOOK AT THIS, DAD.
MY BODY CAN'T TAKE ANYMORE OF THAT MUTT'S TEETH!
IS THERE A WAY TO MAKE WATA UNDERSTAND THAT I'M SUPERIOR TO HIM?
33

OR DO I HAVE TO BEAT HIM UP?
ANYTIME, HUMAN!
YOU HAVE TO ACT DIFFERENTLY.
IF WATA-KUN DOES SOMETHING WRONG...
34

35
...YOU HOLD HIS MUZZLE CAREFULLY LIKE THIS.

36
AND MAKE HIM LIE DOWN.

37
IF YOU REMEMBER TO DO THIS WHEN YOU ARE SCOLDING HIM, HE WILL UNDERSTAND THAT YOU HAVE AUTHORITY OVER HIM.
AND MAKE SURE YOU DON'T SAY HIS NAME WHEN YOU'RE SCOLDING HIM...
OTHERWISE, IT WILL ASSOCIATE ITS NAME WITH A NEGATIVE IMPRESSION.

38
HOLD HIS MUZZLE...

39
...AND MAKE HIM LIE DOWN.

40
IT AIN'T WORKING, DAD! WHY DOES HE LISTEN TO YOU AND NOT *ME*?
うーむ
HMM. I DO NOT KNOW HOW TO PUT IT IN WORDS, BUT...

41
...SOMEHOW I FEEL A SPECIAL AURA FROM YOUR FATHER.
ANYWAY, I WONDER. WHY DOES THIS FAMILY HAVE THE ABILITY TO SPEAK WITH ANIMALS?

42

AND TASUKE'S NAILS…

I CONTEMPLATED WHETHER YOU TWO WERE A FAMILY OF DEMONS…

43

BUT THE AURA I FEEL FROM THE DOCTOR…

ARE *YOU* A MONONOKE, DAD?

44

…IS NOT OF EVIL, BUT IS HOLY AND DIVINE.

WHAT?

OH ♡

45
WHY, THANK YOU, WATA-KUN!
ぱたた
WAG
QUIT WAGGIN' THAT TAIL IN MY FACE!

* THE SHINTO GOD OF DOGS

46

WHAT?

THAT GOLDEN FUR!!

CAN THIS BE? DOCTOR, ARE YOU POSSIBLY THE LEG-ENDARY…

…KOMAINU-SAMA*!?

ふぁさ

THAT IS CORRECT.

47

48
MY GOODNESS!
I AM MOVED BEYOND WORDS!
I WOULD HAVE NEVER IMAGINED THAT A LOWLY MONGREL SUCH AS MYSELF WOULD EVER MEET SUCH A NOBLE AND HONORABLE BEING!
THERE IS NO NEED TO BOW, WATA-KUN.
WHAT THE HELL'S SO GREAT ABOUT MY DAD? HE'S JUST AN OLD MAN!
49
50
FOOL! WATCH YOUR TONGUE! KOMAINU-SAMA IS THE GOD OF DOGS!
YOOOWWEEE!
51
BUT WHY ARE YOU IN HUMAN FORM, KOMAINU-SAMA?
WELL...
IT WAS 20 YEARS AGO...
52

I WAS STILL KOMAINU SERVING THE GOD OF OKUCHI...
HEY, WHAT DO WE DO WITH THE SHRINE?
WE'VE GOTTA LEAVE THE MAIN SHRINE AS IS.
YUP, YUP.
ガガガ
ガガ
PREFECTURAL HIGHWAY CONSTRUCTION
WHAT ABOUT THE KOMAINU?
AH, TAKE IT DOWN.
YUP, YUP.
ヒュウゥゥゥ

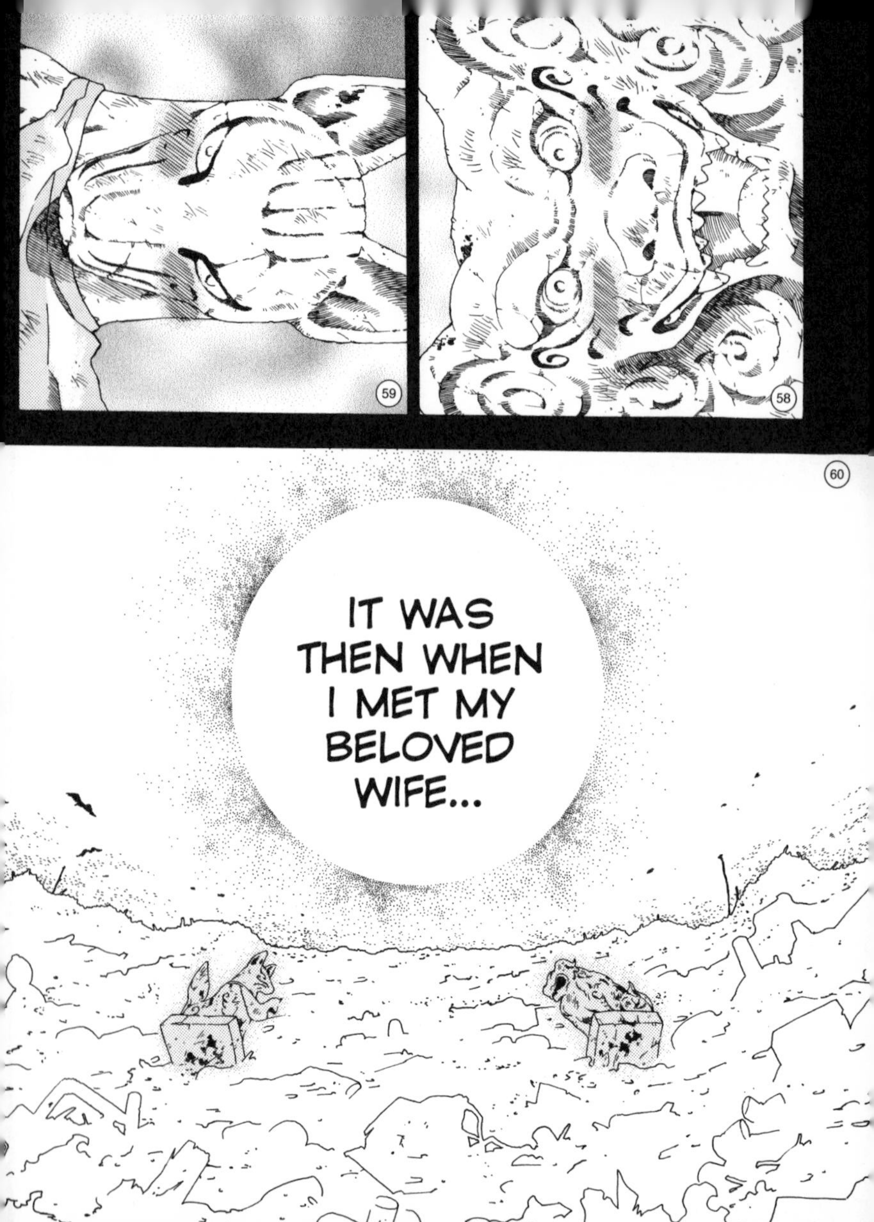
59
58
60
IT WAS THEN WHEN I MET MY BELOVED WIFE...

FROM THERE I BEGAN LIFE ANEW.

HOW TOUCHING.

I TRULY HOPE MY SON WILL MEET THAT SPECIAL SOMEONE AS I HAVE.

I'M NOT GONNA MARRY A STATUE, DAD!

I'M GONNA MARRY A HUMAN BEING!

* THE FOX STATUE THAT USUALLY STANDS IN FRONT OF A SHRINE. OINARI IS A HEAVENLY MESSENGER AND THE GOD OF RICE.

66

HEY, WATA, SINCE MY DAD'S A GOD, AND I'M THE SON OF A GOD...

...THAT MAKES ME HOLY, TOO. SEE, I'M BETTER THAN YOU!

みよ〜〜ん

STRETCH

67

BITE

YOW!
WHAT'RE YOU DOING!?
YOU CAN'T BITE THE SON OF A GOD!
68
THUD!
SILENCE!

69
HOW DARE YOU! YOU KEEP TALKING ABOUT BEING HUMAN, BUT INVOKE THE GODS ONLY WHEN IT IS CONVENIENT.
YOU HAVE NO CLUE HOW IMPORTANT YOUR PARENTS ARE AND YET YOU DISRE-SPECT THEM. YOU, BOY, SHOULD NOT BE CONSIDERED THE SON OF A GOD!
I HAVE NO MERCY FOR BEINGS OF SUCH LOW CALIBER. WHETHER THEY'RE MEN, DOGS OR GODS!

LOW CALIBER ?
YOUR CALIBER HOLDS ABOUT AS MUCH WATER AS A SIEVE!
70

71
わははは
HA HA HA HA! WATA-KUN, THAT WAS VERY WELL SAID.
IT IS AN HONOR TO BE PRAISED BY YOU, KOMAINU-SAMA.
WHY YOU STINK-ING DOG!

WHAT THE HELL'S YOUR PROBLEM, HUH? MAN'S BEST FRIEND, MY ASS!

GUESS I'LL HAVE TO TEACH YOU A LESSON-WITH MY FIST!

BE MY GUEST!

72

73

ガチャ

GOOD MORNING!

74

OH.
WATA, TASUKE-KUN, GOOD MORNING.
わっはっは
HA HA HA! COME 'ERE, BOY!
ふる ふる
WHY'D SHE SAY "GOOD MORNING" TO WATA BEFORE ME?
75

76
WHAT SHOULD I START WITH FIRST, DOCTOR?
WELL, FOR STARTERS, PLEASE PUT ON A UNIFORM.
THEN, PLEASE START BY CLEANING THE IN-PATIENT AREA.
YES, SIR!
WHA? WHAT'S GOING ON?
ぱた ぱた
77

DIDN'T YA HEAR? I'M GONNA START HELPING OUT AROUND THE CLINIC!
IT'S THE LEAST I CAN DO FOR TAKING CARE OF WATA.
HUH?
I TOLD HER NOT TO WORRY ABOUT IT, WITH EXAMS COMING AND ALL.
79
78

MISATO-SAN SAYS SHE WANTS TO BECOME A VET.
IF THAT IS THE CASE, PERHAPS SHE CAN LEARN A FEW THINGS BY HELPING OUT AROUND THE CLINIC.
80

IF ONLY MY OWN SON FELT THE WAY SHE DID!
WHAT CAN SHE POSSIBLY LEARN IN A DUMP LIKE THIS?
THERE'RE HARDLY ANY IN-PATIENTS.
81

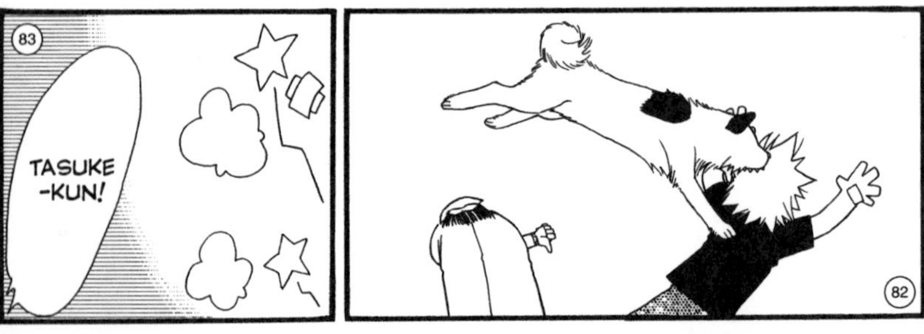
82
TASUKE -KUN!
83

YES, SEN-PAI?
TASUKE-KUN, WILL YOU CLEAN THAT SIDE OF THE ROOM?
YOU'RE ALREADY CHANGED!
WHAT?
84

85
AND AFTER THAT, PLEASE REARRANGE THE SHELVES.
HUH?
ME, TOO?
86
HM? DID YOU SAY SOMETHING?
NO, NO. NOTHING. WHERE'S THE BROOM? HA HA!
へらへら
......
87
HE TRULY IS A BEING OF LOW CALIBER.
IT SEEMS THE RANKING HAS BEEN FIXED.

88

AH, THAT IS PRE-CISELY IT!

LEADER MISATO

GOD KOMAINU

SUPERIOR WATA

INFERIOR TASUKE

GAUGAU WATA ガウガウわー太
BOW WOW WATA
TM

CHAPTER 5: WHEN A BLACK CAT CROSSES YOUR PATH

KYAAAAH!
2

3
WHAT IS IT, KYOKO?
A BLACK CAT!

やだー
YOU KNOW WHAT THEY SAY: IT'S BAD LUCK IF A BLACK CAT CROSSES YOUR PATH!
きゃはは
HA HA HA!
4

SO I'M A BLACK CAT! BIG DEAL!
WEIRDOS!
5

WHENEVER I WALK PAST A HUMAN...
...THEY ALWAYS SAY I'M BAD LUCK.

I CAN'T BELIEVE THEY FALL FOR SUPERSTITIONS!
STUPID HUMANS!

“BAD LUCK”.

ぴく
TWITCH
!
かじかじ
SCRATCH, SCRATCH
ITCHY, ITCHY!

ろ動物病院

HEY!

A CAT!

DON'T YOU KNOW? THEY SAY THAT BAD THINGS HAPPEN TO YOU IF A BLACK CAT CROSSES YOUR PATH!
BAD LUCK?

....
YOU HUMANS HOLD SOME RATHER STRANGE BELIEFS.

HUH? THIS CAT...
....

COME, KITTY, KITTY...
MEOW.
MEOW.
MEOW.
SHE'S TRYING TO TALK CAT.

WAIT A SEC. I'VE GOT SOME SNACKS HERE SOME-WHERE...
NOW WHERE IS IT?

HERE YOU GO!

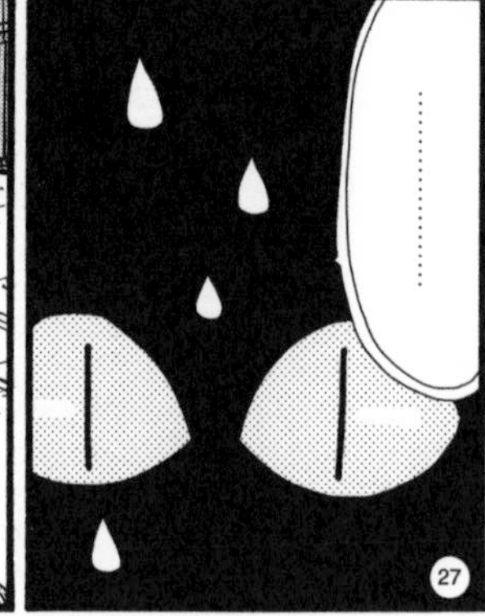

......

ぴゅ

かーーッ
WHAT THE HELL'S THAT CAT'S PROBLEM?
IGNORING MISATO-SENPAI WHEN SHE WAS JUST BEING NICE!
IT'S OK, TASUKE-KUN. IT'S A STRAY. IT CAN'T HELP ITSELF.

BUT...
...THERE'S SOME-THING ABOUT THAT CAT...

WHAT WAS THAT ALL ABOUT?
WHO WAS THAT GIRL?
WHY DIDN'T SHE ACT ALL HYSTERICAL LIKE THE OTHER HUMANS?

....

WEIRD.

THAT GIRL...

... DOES SHE LIVE IN THAT HOUSE?

GOOD MORNING!

HUH?

IT'S THAT CAT AGAIN! WHAT DOES IT WANT NOW?
MAYBE IT CAME TO PLAY!

MEOW ...
MEOW ...

SHE'S **DEFINITELY** WEIRD.
SHE'S NOT LIKE THE OTHER HUMANS...

MISATO-SENPAI, YOU SHOULDN'T.
IT COULD HAVE RABIES.

TWITCH
TASUKE-KUN!
UH... YES?

HOW CAN YOU BE SO MEAN?

DO YOU HAVE SOMETHING AGAINST CATS?

NO... I'M SORRY.
CATS ARE ADORABLE. HA HA...
WHAT THE? WHO ARE THESE PEOPLE?

SNAP
パ
OH YEAH...YOU KNOW HOW YOU SAID YOU NEVER EAT BREAKFAST? WELL, I MADE SOME SANDWICHES. HOPE YOU LIKE 'EM.
WHAT!?
HANDMADE, HANDMADE
手作り 手作り

がーん
HERE, KITTY, KITTY. YOU CAN HAVE HALF OF TASUKE-KUN'S SANDWICH!
48

I'VE GOTTA SHARE IT WITH THE CAT? THAT STUPID, GOOD FOR NOTHING, STRAY!
YOU ARE BEING CHILDISH.
WELL, I'LL LEAVE IT HERE, SO EAT UP, OK, KITTY?
ゴゴゴゴ
49
50

C'MON, CAT! EAT IT! OR WHAT, ARE YOU SAYING MISATO-SENPAI'S SANDWICH ISN'T GOOD ENOUGH?
CALM DOWN, TASUKE-KUN. IT'S JUST BEING CAREFUL.
そうかもしれないけど。
ヤケ
51

WE'D BETTER GO.
COME, WATA.
RUFF!
わん
52

HEY, SENPAI, WHAT'RE YOU GONNA DO WITH THAT OTHER HALF OF THE SANDWICH?
I'LL GIVE IT TO YOU LATER. IT'S IMPOLITE TO EAT AND WALK AT THE SAME TIME.
53

YAY! IT ATE MY SAND-WICH!
BUT I WONDER WHY IT'S STILL HERE?
ぼそ
STILL HERE? SHEESH!

61
HEY, WATA, TELL THAT CAT TO GET THE HELL OUT OF HERE!

62
WHY?
ARE YOU JEALOUS OF THE CAT?

ちッ
NO!
IT'S JUST STARTING TO ANNOY ME, THAT'S ALL!
63
IT IS A STRAY, TASUKE.

64
THE CAT IS FREE TO GO WHEREVER IT WANTS.
IT IS A BAD HABIT OF HUMANS TO TRY AND TAKE CONTROL OF EVERYTHING.

BUT MY SANDWICH ...
ブー
SANDWICH?
OH YEAH!
65

66
MAYBE IT WASN'T ENOUGH!
HERE! HAVE THE OTHER HALF!
ギャース
WHAT ABOUT ME !?

67

68

ぴゅ

69

70

LOOK WHAT MISATO-SAN MADE FOR ME...A SANDWICH!

まぐ

MUNCH

ぐーきゅるる

GROWWL!

71

75

"BAD LUCK".

76

THAT'S WHAT THE HUMANS SAY ABOUT ME.

I GOT SO USED TO BEING CALLED THAT THAT I STARTED PLAYING TRICKS ON THEM.

BUT THAT GIRL...

77
78
THAT SANDWICH SURE WAS GOOD.
WHAT A WEIRDO.

BUT MAYBE IT'S ME THAT CHANGING...

ばん!
HEY! COME BACK HERE WITH OUR DINNER!
83
WHAT'S UP, DAD?
AAAAGGH!
84
ばりばりばり
SCREECH! HISS!
85
86
OUR DINNER... GONE.
......
WHY THAT STUPID BLACK CAT! WHAT'S THE BIG IDEA!? I'M GONNA KILL IT!
ぐす
(SIGH) DINNER... GONE...
87
I'M SORRY, TASUKE. YOU WILL HAVE TO SETTLE WITH JUST RICE.
88
SO THAT FISH WAS *MINE*, HUH?
ぽん

GOOD MORNING.
I BROUGHT YOU SOME BREAKFAST.
SOME GRATED DRIED BONITO AND CRAB-FLAVORED FISH CAKES.
I HOPE YOU LIKE 'EM.
ひょこ

IT'S OK.

HERE, HAVE SOME FISH CAKES! COME ON, IT'S OK.

THIS GIRL...
...MAYBE SHE'S DIFFERENT...

GAUGAU WATA ガウガウわー太
BOW WOW WATA
TM

CHAPTER 6: WA-TAN

STU-
PID
BLACK
CAT...

WHY'S IT FOLLOWING US?
8
THAT CAT BETTER NOT BE GOING AFTER MISATO-SENPAI!
YOU'RE SO CUTE, KURO-CHAN!
DON'T YOU THINK SO, TOO, WATA?
RUFF!
わん
ゴゴゴ
9
10
HUH!
KURO-CHAN?
11
あっ
THAT'S A GREAT NAME! AND EASY TO REMEMBER, TOO!
12
I WONDER IF THAT NAME'S OK? IS IT TOO OBVIOUS?
13
KURO...
MY NAME'S...
KURO!

OH, I ALMOST FORGOT.
HERE, TASUKE-KUN.
HERE, YOU CAN HAVE IT BACK.
ISN'T THIS THE FISH KURO-CHAN TOOK FROM YOU YESTERDAY?
MY DINNER!

ポツ
ポ

(SIGH) I HATE THE RAIN!

DON'T LET IT GET TO YOU, TASUKE-KUN. CHEER UP!

I BROUGHT ENOUGH FOOD FOR ALL OF US TODAY.

I HOPE YOU ALL LIKE IT!

HUH!?

FOR *EVERYONE* !?

YUP. HERE, THIS RICE BALL'S FOR YOU, TASUKE-KUN.

じーーーん
SHE MADE THIS... JUST FOR ME!
YE... YESSS!
HUH?
WHO DOES HE THINK HE IS!?
THAT GIRL MADE THAT RICE BALL FOR ME!
ひょい!
MINE!
!!!!

HEY, KURO-CHAN!
THAT'S NOT YOURS!
たたた
HE'S DEAD!
GET OVER HERE!
どぉー
TASUKE-KUN, COME BACK! I HAVE ANOTHER RICE BALL RIGHT HERE!
C'MON! KURO-CHAN'LL COME BACK TO THE CLINIC LATER ANYWAY!
BUT... I GUESS YOU CAN'T HEAR ME NOW...
WHY DOES HE ALWAYS OVERRE-ACT?

DR. YASHIRO ...
...CAN YOU PLEASE FEED KURO-CHAN WHEN SHE GETS BACK?
I WILL. THANK YOU, MISATO-SAN.

SEE YOU LATER, THEN.
TAKE CARE.

MUNCH, MUNCH
はぐ
はぐ
KURO-CHAN!
YOU KNOW IT'S NOT GOOD TO TAKE OTHER PEOPLE'S FOOD, RIGHT?

WELL?
ぱた
I'LL TAKE THAT WAG AS A "YES."
NOW YOU BE GOOD.

THERE'S GOTTA BE SOME-THING WRONG WITH ME.
THERE'S SOMETHING ABOUT THIS GIRL...
I CAN'T BELIEVE I RESPONDED TO A HUMAN...
WHAT'S GOING ON?
THERE IS NOTHING WRONG WITH YOU, KURO-DONO.
STARE
じ
HUH!
はっ
ばっ
I TOOK THIS FROM THAT KID, SO IT'S MINE! YOU CAN'T HAVE ANY!
YOU DON'T KNOW WHAT IT'S LIKE TO BE A STRAY, YOU HOUSE DOG!
I AM NOT GOING TO TAKE YOUR RICE BALL.
DO NOT WORRY.
I WAS JUST THINKING HOW MISATO-DONO HAS GROWN...

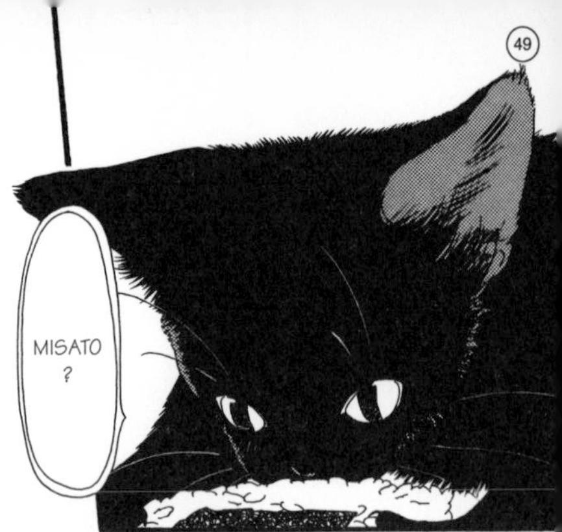
MISATO
?

IS THAT THE GIRL'S NAME?
……

HEY, MISTER, YOU SAID THAT THERE'S NOTHING WRONG WITH ME…
BUT THERE IS! I'VE NEVER FELT LIKE THIS BEFORE!
I **HATE** HUMANS! BUT…
BUT …

THAT IS CORRECT.

MISATO-DONO IS A HUMAN BEING.

BUT SHE IS SPECIAL.

SPECIAL ?

……

サァァア

HEY, A STRAY PUPPY!
MOMMY, LET'S TAKE IT HOME. I PROMISE I'LL TAKE CARE OF IT.
NO, YUTA!
AND JUST LOOK AT HIM! HE DOESN'T LOOK FRIENDLY.
HE LOOKS SCARY.
ひょい
REALLY?
YOU'RE RIGHT. HE DOESN'T YELP AT ALL.
WHAT'RE YOU DOING, BIG BROTHER?
DOGS THAT DON'T YELP WHEN YOU HOLD THEM BY THE NECK ARE STRONG, YOU KNOW!
COOL! HE'S STRONG? THEN LET'S TAKE HIM HOME!
I SAID NO!! HE MIGHT GROW UP TO BE A MEAN DOG.
MUMBLE, MUMBLE
ぶつぶつ
FINE.
......
ぐ～きゅるるる
GROWWL!

WA-TAN!
MOMMY! A WA-TAN!
* EDITOR'S NOTE: WAN-CHAN IS MOST FREQUENTLY USED BY YOUNG CHILDREN TO REFER TO DOGS.
HEY, HEY, IT'S NOT A WA-TAN, IT'S A WAN-CHAN*!
くすくす
(GIGGLE) I THINK THAT'S WHAT MISATO'S TRYING TO SAY.
WA-TAN, WA-TAN!
WE'RE NOT GOING TO TAKE THIS ONE HOME, MISATO.
OUR HOUSE IS ALREADY FILLED WITH STRAYS YOU'VE BROUGHT HOME!
ALTHOUGH WE BOUGHT SOME FROM THE PET STORE...
SO NO MORE ANIMALS, PLEASE.
WA-TAN!
WE'RE GOING HOME, MISATO.
......
ぐーきゅる
GROWWL!

74
きゅるる
GROWWL
ぐう
75
76
ぐーきゅる
GROWWL
たたたた
たたたた
77
たた
78
HERE, WA-TAN!
79
80
GOOD BOY, GOOD BOY.
81
82

BYE, BYE!
たたたた
……
MUNCH
もぐ
ばら
……
MUNCH
もぐ
MUNCH
もぐ
むしゃ
MUNCH
HEY, LOOK. IT'S A STRAY.

ギャハハ
I BET NO ONE WANTS TO TAKE IT HOME!
HA HA HA!
NO WONDER. IT'S FILTHY!
IT'LL PROBABLY GROW UP TO BE SOME FUNKY DOG! HEY, WHY DON'T WE HAVE SOME FUN WITH IT?
HA HA HA!
アハハ
HAVE FUN WITH IT? WHAT'RE WE GONNA DO?
I'VE GOT SOMETHIN' THAT'LL MAKE THIS DOG EVEN BETTER.
HUH? WHAT IS IT?
A STAPLER?

98
サァァァ
99
たたたた
100
たたた
101
102
WA-TAN!
103
ばしゃ
104
ばしゃ
ばしゃ
105
WA-TAN!!
ばしゃ

ばしゃばしゃ
谷川動物病院
DOCTOR !
DOCTOR, PLEA HELP WA-TAN!
SO MUCH BLOOD! HE GONNA DIE!
MY GOOD-NESS !!
HOW CRUEL... SOMEBODY STAPLED HIS EAR.
DOCTOR, PLEA HELP WA-TAN!
ME DO CHORES AND GIVE YOU MONEY!
PLEA ...
PLEA!
えっえっ

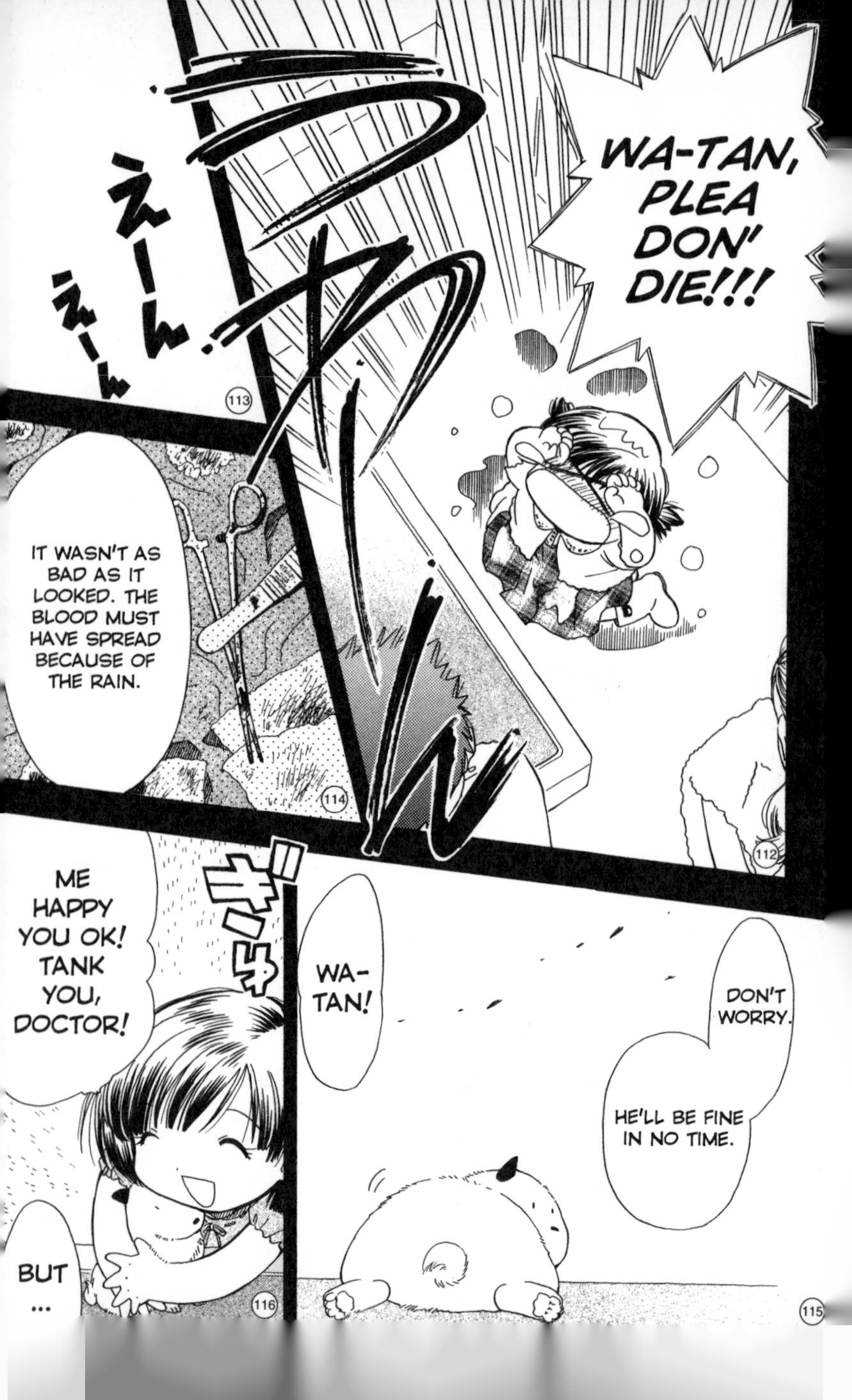
WA-TAN, PLEA DON' DIE!!!
えーん
えーん
IT WASN'T AS BAD AS IT LOOKED. THE BLOOD MUST HAVE SPREAD BECAUSE OF THE RAIN.
DON'T WORRY.
HE'LL BE FINE IN NO TIME.
WA-TAN!
ME HAPPY YOU OK! TANK YOU, DOCTOR!
BUT ...

117
...A NERVE IN HIS LEFT EAR SEEMS TO HAVE BEEN DAMAGED SO IT'LL PROBABLY STAY FLAT.
118
119
FLAT EAR...
...NO FIX?
120
OK!
121
WA-TAN, ME GONNA BE DOCTOR AND FIX EAR!
ME PROMISE!
122
OH, SO YOU'RE GOING TO BE A VET, MISATO-CHAN?
YOU'D BETTER STUDY HARD AT SCHOOL.
ME WILL!
123
WA-TAN, IT PROMISE!
LINK FINGERS FOR PROMISE.
124
....
OH NO FINGER...

I KNOW!
SHAKE HAND!
ME FIX, OK, WA-TAN?
MISATO-DONO IS MY ONLY MASTER.
WA-TAN!
AND ONLY LADY MISA-TO.
WA-TAN!
WATA!
SO THAT GIRL, MISATO, IS SPECIAL...
...HUH?
サァァァ

GAUGAU WATA ガウガウわた
BOW WOW WATA TM

CHAPTER 7: THE DUEL

サァァァァ
THAT'S WEIRD ...
I WONDER IF THAT BLACK CAT'S HER'S?
みゅ!
MEOW
みゅー
MEOW
ぐす
MOMMY, I'M SCARED!
にゃあ
MEOW
にゃあ
MEOW
にゃあ
MEOW
WHERE AM I?
カリ
カリ
I WANNA GO HOME.
MOMMY.

GRR...
グルル…
9

WHAT
DID I DO?

WHY
ME?

IF I'VE BEEN
A BAD KITTY,
I'M SORRY!

PLEASE...

12

17
MOMMY ...

18

19
WHEN A HUMAN BEING ABANDONS THEIR PET, IT IS EQUIVALENT TO KILLING THAT ANIMAL.
BUT IN ORDER TO AVOID FEELING GUILTY OF LITERALLY KILLING AN ANIMAL...
...HUMANS OPT TO ABANDON THEM SOMEWHERE—SOME-WHERE FAR SO THEY DO NOT HAVE TO THINK ABOUT WHAT THEY HAVE DONE...
...HOPING THAT SOMEONE ELSE WILL ADOPT THE ABANDONED ANIMAL. FOOLISH, HUMAN BEINGS ARE.

20
I WILL...
...NEVER FORGET AND FORGIVE WHAT HUMANS DID TO ME.

21
....
MISTER, YOU...

22
BUT A HUMAN BEING ALSO HELPED ME.

ALTHOUGH SHE IS HUMAN, MISATO-DONO IS INDEED SPECIAL.
...AND ONLY MISATO-DONO.
IF ONLY I'D MET THAT MISATO EARLIER...
...THEN...
IT DOES NOT MATTER WHEN YOU MET HER. WHAT IS IMPORTANT IS THAT YOU DID.
YOU CAN BEGIN LIFE ANEW STARTING TODAY.

I HAVE DECIDED TO DEVOTE MY LIFE TO MISATO-DONO.
I WILL PROTECT MISATO-DONO FROM HARMS WAY FOR AS LONG AS I LIVE!

WATA-SAN... NO, PLEASE LET ME CALL YOU BROTHER WATA!
OH, BUT KURO-DONO, IS IT FITTING TO CALL **ME** BROTHER?

IS BROTHER NO GOOD? THEN I'LL CALL YOU **MASTER**!
PLEASE LET ME PROTECT MISATO-SAMA, TOO!
....

MASTER, LET ME MASSAGE YOUR SHOULDERS!
......
A-HA! THERE YOU ARE!

HUF
ぜー
HUF
はー
HUH?
AHHHHH!
GLARE
WHY YOU...

ぶん
SWING
WHY'RE YOU ALWAYS SNOOPING AROUND MY HOUSE?
GET OUTTA HERE!
ぶん
SHUT UP, HUMAN!
HITACHI
たん!
しぱっ
THIS IS MY TERRITORY!
SO YOU GET OUTTA HERE!
OW!

YOU PIECE OF BAD LUCK! THIS IS *MY* HOUSE!
YOUR TERRITORY? DON'T THINK SO, PAL!

HUH?
HOW DOES HE KNOW WHAT I JUST SAID?
......

HUH!
はっ
WHAT? I DIDN'T HEAR *ANYTHING*!
うきゃー
JUST GET OUTTA HERE, WILL YA!

GRAB
かしっ
CONGRAT-ULATIONS, TASUKE!! WE MUST CELEBRATE!!
AAARRRRGH!!

HE IS BEGINNING TO UNDERSTAND THE LANGUAGE OF ANIMALS! WE HAVE AN ANIMAL COUN-SELOR IN THE MAKING! DANCE WITH ME, WATA-KUN!
I ONLY KNOW THE TANGO...
WHY?
WHY DOES THIS HAPPEN TO ME? WHY, OF ALL THINGS, DID I HAVE TO UNDERSTAND THAT STUPID BLACK CAT?

STUPID BLACK CAT?

TAKE BACK WHAT YOU SAID, HUMAN! I AM MASTER WATA'S TRUSTED SIDEKICK!
BITE
OW OW OW OW!

MASTER, WHAT SHOULD I DO WITH THIS CONCEITED HUMAN?
KURO-DONO, THERE IS NO NEED TO CALL ME MASTER...
PERHAPS I WAS TOO LOOSE ON TEACHING MY SON MANNERS...
SCREW YOU ALL!

CALM DOWN, TASUKE ♥
LOOK WHAT I HAVE FOR YOU. MISATO-SAN ASKED ME TO GIVE THIS TO YOU.

YES! FINALLY I GET TO HAVE MISATO-SENPAI'S HOMEMADE RICE BALL!

HUH?

DRIED SARDINES?

BUT THIS RICE BALL LOOKS LIKE IT WAS MADE FOR A CAT.
IT'S SMALL, TOO.
OF COURSE IT DOES. MISATO-SAN MADE IT FOR KURO-SAN.

FOR KURO?

FOR ME?

THAT'S MINE!

KEEP YOUR PAWS OFF MY FOOD, HUMAN!

OH!
....
GULP

62
M-M-MY... RICE... BALL...
ふるふるふる
MISATO-SENPAI'S...
63
I WONDER IF TASUKE-KUN WILL LIKE IT ♥ HEE HEE ♥
...RICE BALL.
HE'S DEAD!
TASUKE, IT'S FOR KURO-SAN, NOT YOU...

64
ザッ
どたたたたたたた
65
がさがさ
TASUKE, STOP RIGHT THIS INSTANT!
66
だだだだだだた
67
HEY, KURO!

68

69
THIS FISH ...
YEAH, IT'S THE FISH YOU STOLE FROM ME.
70

71
PICK IT UP!
I DARE YOU!

72

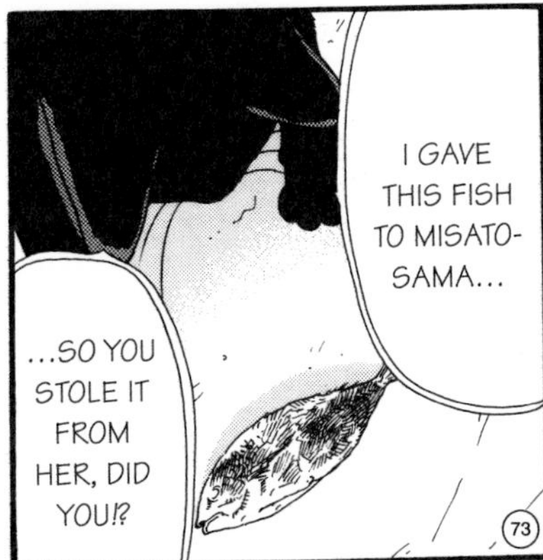
I GAVE THIS FISH TO MISATO-SAMA...
...SO YOU STOLE IT FROM HER, DID YOU!?
73

74
ばく
YOU'LL PAY FOR THIS!

ザァァァァ
75

76
77

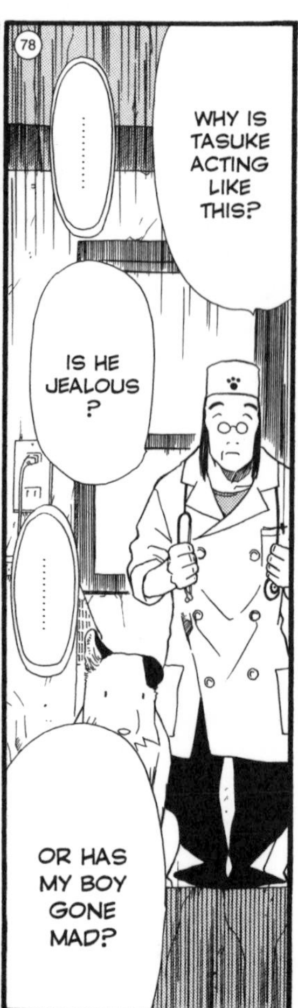
78
......
WHY IS TASUKE ACTING LIKE THIS?
IS HE JEALOUS?
......
OR HAS MY BOY GONE MAD?

79
IF I WIN THIS FIGHT, YOU BACK AWAY FROM MISATO-SENPAI!
AND NO GOING BACK ON A MAN-TO-MAN PROMISE, GOT IT?

HUMPH! *YOU'D* BETTER NOT BACK DOWN ON THIS PROMISE, HUMAN!
I ACCEPT YOUR CHALLENGE! NO MERCY!
80

81
......
TASUKE, THERE IS SOMETHING I MUST TELL YOU BEFORE YOU TWO FIGHT…

KURO-DONO IS FEMALE.

COME AGAIN?

ザァー
TASUKE!
DRY UP AND CHANGE! YOU HAVE SCHOOL TO ATTEND!

CHAPTER 8: BAD LUCK

KURO-CHAN ...
... I CAN'T WALK WITH YOU THIS CLOSE TO ME.
AH...
へっくしょ
AH-CHOO!

7
OH, TASUKE-KUN, DID YOU CATCH A COLD?
ずー
8
ぴゅ
9
MORNIN', MISATO!
10
OH, HEY, HANA!
11

TASUKE-KUN, THIS IS OIKAWA HANAKO. WE'RE CLASS-MATES.
MORN-ING!

GOOD MORNING, I'M YASHIRO TASUKE.
HMM.

SO IS THIS YOUR BOYFRIEND FROM THE ANIMAL CLINIC? HE'S CUTE.
CUT IT OUT, HANA! THAT'S NOT NICE!
NEVER KNEW MISATO-SENPAI THOUGHT ABOUT ME THAT WAY...
ぶん
ぶん
B... BOY-FRIEND!

HE'S LIKE MY LITTLE BROTHER!
RIGHT, TASUKE-KUN?
ぺし

OH REALLY? WELL, THERE IS THAT OTHER GUY...

WHAT'S HIS NAME AGAIN?
KYAAH!
きゃー

むんず

HEY, MR. UNLUCKY. STAY AWAY FROM MISATO-SENPAI!

WHAT DID YOU SAY!? I'VE GOTTA PROTECT MISATO-SAMA WHEN MASTER WATA IS UNABLE TO.

ズびし

OUTTA MY WAY, **LITTLE BROTHER!**

たったったった

THAT CAT'S SO STUBBORN...
GRRRR!
ぶへーっくしょん
AH CHOO!
ポン
HERE YA GO!

ピー

NOW, PRACTICE IN PAIRS!

MAKE SURE YOU DON'T LEAVE THE BALLS LYING AROUND. IT CAN BE DANGEROUS.

はーい

YES, MA'AM!

MISATO-SENPAI...

...SHE'S SO CUTE!

ずびー

NOTHING'S GONE RIGHT EVER SINCE THAT BLACK CAT SHOWED UP!
FIRST, IT STOLE MY DINNER. THEN I UNDERSTAND WHAT IT SAYS. NOW, I'VE EVEN GOT A COLD!
BLACK CATS REALLY ARE UNLUCKY!

THERE'S OIKAWA-SENPAI.
OH YEAH, THEY'RE IN THE SAME CLASS...
WELL, THERE IS THAT OTHER GUY...
KYAAH!

WAIT A SEC...

IT CAN'T BE!

DOES SHE ALREADY HAVE A BOYFRIEND!?

UH, YASHIRO-KUN, DO YOU HAVE A QUES-TION?
UH... WHAT?
NO, SIR.
HUH?

ガタ
ガタ
WHAT A KLUTZ. SHE TRIPPED OVER THE BALL.
HEY, SHE'S PRETTY CUTE!
ざわ

DING!
キーン
DONG!
コーン

THIRD-YEAR FUNAKOSHI-SAN?
SHE'S NOT HERE.
BUT I HEARD SHE GOT HURT DURING GYM AND CAME HERE.
INFIRMARY
保健室
WELL, SHE DID.
BUT...
I HAD SOMEONE PICK HER UP BECAUSE IT LOOKED MORE SERIOUS THAN AN ANKLE SPRAIN.
MISATO-SENPAI!
SMACK!
!!

TASUKE, HOW IS MISATO-SAMA?
SHE'S STILL IN THAT ROOM, ISN'T SHE?
IT'S ALL *YOUR* FAULT!

BUT I... I WAS JUST TRYING TO PROTECT MISATO-SAMA...
WITH YOU HANGING AROUND, MISATO-SENPAI'S NOT SAFE!

BLACK CATS ARE BAD LUCK!!

SO STAY AWAY FROM HER! GOT IT!?
ピシャ!
SLAM!

"BAD LUCK".

....

MAN, I THINK I HAVE A FEVER!
OH, THERE YOU ARE, TASUKE-KUN.

OIKAWA-SENPAI!
YOU'RE SO FORMAL! JUST CALL ME HANA ♥

UH, HANA-SENPAI ...

MISATO SAID TO TELL YOU THAT SHE'D CALL YOU LATER.
AND THAT ...
HEY, HANA, C'MON!
OH, SORRY, GOTTA RUN!

SEE YA!
....
SO HOW'S MISATO-SENPAI?

じり
じり
....
STUPID CAT...
...MISATO-SENPAI'S NOT THERE ANYMORE.

74
MAYBE I'LL TELL HER...
75
76
... NAH!
くる
77
IT'S ALL HER FAULT THAT SENPAI'S HURT! NO WAY I'M GONNA TELL HER!
SHE'LL PROBABLY GIVE UP SOON AND COME TO THE CLINIC AGAIN...
JUST LEAVE HER.
78
79
ゴロ
ゴロ
ゴロ
80
ガッ
81
ザ

82
REALLY?
ずびばはは
I'M GLAD IT'S NOTHING SERIOUS!

83
YEAH...BUT IT'S SPRAINED SO I DON'T THINK I CAN WALK WATA FOR A WHILE...

84
DON'T WORRY ABOUT WATA! LEAVE IT TO ME AND TAKE CARE OF THAT SPRAIN!
I WOULD LIKE TO SPEAK TO MISATO-DONO AS WELL.
わんわん
RUFF, RUFF!

85
IS THAT WATA BARKING? HEY, TASUKE-KUN, CAN YOU PUT WATA ON?

86
IT'S FOR YOU...

87
ぱたぱた
クーン

88
BY THE WAY, TASUKE-KUN...
ばッ
YES ♥

89
...IT'S ABOUT KURO-CHAN...
YES?

SHE'S THERE, RIGHT? CAN YOU GIVE HER SOMETHING TO EAT?

I KNOW YOU'RE SICK, AND I HATE TO ASK YOU, BUT PLEASE.
90

NO PROBLEM! I'LL MAKE SURE KURO GETS FED.

91
CLICK
カチャ

ALWAYS PUTTING ANIMALS BEFORE HERSELF...
92

...I'M SURE SHE'LL MAKE A GREAT VET ONE DAY...

93

94
....

ガラ
HEY, KURO! DINNER!
YOU SHOULD BE GRATE-FUL!
CAT FOOD
95

96

97
ザー
ゴロゴロゴロ
IT IS STARTING TO RAIN HEAVY …
IT IS SAID THAT CATS DISLIKE WATER. KURO-DONO MUST HAVE TAKEN SHELTER ELSEWHERE.

98
WAIT A SEC...
TAKEN SHELTER?
IS SHE STILL THERE?

99
TASUKE !?
ダッ

100
TASUKE !
バシャバシャ

101
FOOLISH BOY. YOU ARE NOT FIT TO GO OUT IN THE RAIN.
VERY WELL. I SHALL ACCOMPANY YOU.

102
SHE'S STILL NOT THERE, IS SHE?
SHE'S GOTTA BE SOMEWHERE ELSE.

103
BUT...
...IS SHE?
AND WHY?
ゴロゴロゴロ

104
105
ザー
106
107
むんず
SIGH
108
109
CRAZY CAT.
YOU'RE SO STUPID.

GAUGAU WATA
ガウガウわー太
BOW WOW WATA
TM

CHAPTER 9:
GRAINS OF RICE
1

SHE IS SUFFERING FROM HEAT-STROKE.
2
3

IT IS NOT GOOD TO BE OUT IN THE SUN TOO LONG DURING THIS SEASON.
KURO-SAN'S BLACK HAIR ABSORBS SUNLIGHT, TOO.
5

4
IT WAS GOOD SHE WAS COOLED IN THE EVENING SHOWER.

I WILL KEEP AN EYE ON HER, BUT I THINK SHE WILL BE OK.
GOOD.
BUT DAD...
6

...I'M SICK, TOO. AREN'T YOU WORRIED ABOUT ME?
YOU WILL BE FINE IN NO TIME.
7

ANYWAY, PLEASE TAKE WATA-KUN FOR A WALK.
AH-CHOO!
ゴホ COUGH
HEY, WATA.
THAT CAT...KURO. SHE'S A GOOD CAT, RIGHT?
SHE TRIED TO PROTECT MISATO-SENPAI, EVEN WHEN SHE WAS SUFFERING FROM HEAT-STROKE...
I SHOULD'VE TOLD KURO THE TRUTH.
WHAT'S WRONG WITH ME?

GOOD MORNING.

OH, MISATO-SAN. IF YOU ARE LOOKING FOR WATA-KUN, HE'S OUT ON HIS WALK.

HOW IS YOUR ANKLE DOING?

IT'S A LOT BETTER NOW, BUT IT STILL HURTS WHEN I WALK.

I LEFT MY HOUSE EARLY SO I WON'T BE LATE FOR SCHOOL.

ANY-WAY, UM...

I...
... BROUGHT THIS...

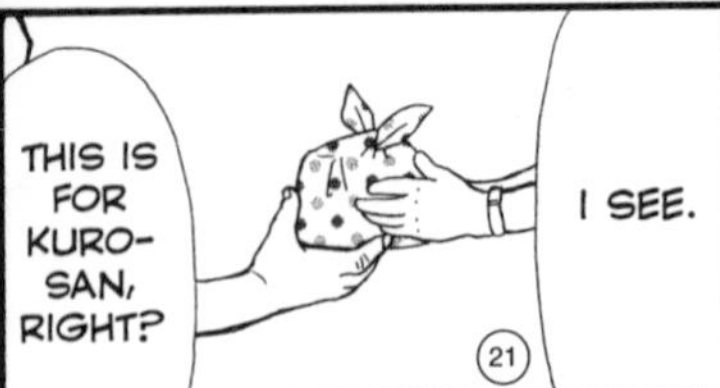
I SEE.
THIS IS FOR KURO-SAN, RIGHT?

BY THE WAY, MISATO-SAN.

IT WAS VERY CLEVER OF YOU TO MIX *THAT* IN WITH KURO-SAN'S MEAL.
!

DOCTOR... HOW DID YOU KNOW?

KURO-SAN IS ALWAYS SCRATCHING HER BEHIND.

がじがじ

SCRATCH, SCRATCH

IT USUALLY ITCHES THERE WHEN CATS HAVE FLEAS.

25

THE SAME GOES FOR OTHER ANIMALS AS WELL.

BUT I AM VERY IMPRESSED! YOU ARE SO PERCEPTIVE!

26

27

MISATO-SAMA'S VOICE.

28

MISATO-SAMA!

29

I'M SORRY.
I'M SORRY I COULDN'T PROTECT YOU.
I COULDN'T DO ANYTHING.
30
MASTER WATA, I HAVE FAILED YOU!
31
32
WITH YOU HANGING AROUND, MISATO-SENPAI'S NOT SAFE!
33
BLACK CATS ARE BAD LUCK!!
34

IT'S...
... IT'S ALL MY FAULT!
!
BARF!
......
WHAT'S GOIN' ON?
I FEEL WEIRD...
うえっ
ケッ
AM I ...
... GONNA DIE!?

ゴホ ゲホ
COUGH
COUGH
I'M HOME.
41

HEY, DAD. I'M TOO SICK TO GO TO SCHOOL TODAY...
CAN YOU GIVE 'EM A CALL?
CERTAINLY.
BUT BEFORE YOU GO TO BED, PLEASE TAKE THIS TO KURO-SAN.
42

43

WHAT'S THIS?
44

WAS MISATO-SENPAI HERE!?
YES. SHE SAYS SHE IS SORRY FOR NOT BEING ABLE TO WALK WATA-KUN.
45

I'VE STILL GOT TIME TO CATCH UP TO HER!

だッ

HEY, DAD, FORGET ABOUT THAT CALL! I'M GONNA GIVE KURO HER FOOD AND GO TO SCHOOL!

VERY WELL. BUT I THOUGHT YOU WERE FEELING ILL...

KURO! FOOD!

バン!

…ワナ
WHAT A SIGHT.
THAT STUPID CAT. WHY'D SHE DO THIS FOR?
LOOK AT THIS PLACE. IT'S A *MESS!*
HUH?

55
56
WHAT'S THIS? GRAINS OF RICE?
SOME OF 'EM ARE DRIED UP AND YELLOW.
乾燥して黄色くなってるのもある
DID SHE ALREADY EAT MISATO-SENPAI'S FOOD?

57
TASUKE!! DO NOT PUT THOSE IN YOUR MOUTH!
どーん

HEY! DO YOU THINK I'D EAT AFTER A CAT?
TASUKE, THOSE ARE NOT GRAINS OF RICE.
THOSE ARE THE PROGLOTTIDS OF A DIPYLIDIUM CANINUM.
BECAUSE OF YOU, THEY ALMOST POPPED INTO MY MOUTH.
58

ガビーーーン

DIPYLIDIUM CANINUM
(DOG TAPEWORM)

A PARASITIC TAPEWORM WHICH ATTACHES ITSELF ON TO THE WALLS OF THE SMALL INTESTINES OF DOGS AND CATS. LENGTH: 15-80 CM, WIDTH 2-3 MM. PROGLOTTIDS ARE DISCHARGED FROM THE BODY THROUGH THE ANIMAL'S FECES, WHERE SEGMENTS ARE SWALLOWED BY LARVAL FLEAS. IT IS THROUGH THESE FLEAS THAT THE ANIMAL IS INFECTED WITH THE TAPEWORM. A PROGLOTTID LOOKS LIKE A GRAIN OF RICE, IS CUCURBITACEOUS AND FRUIT-SHAPED, AND CONTAINS EGGS.

片節
A PROGLOTTID

59

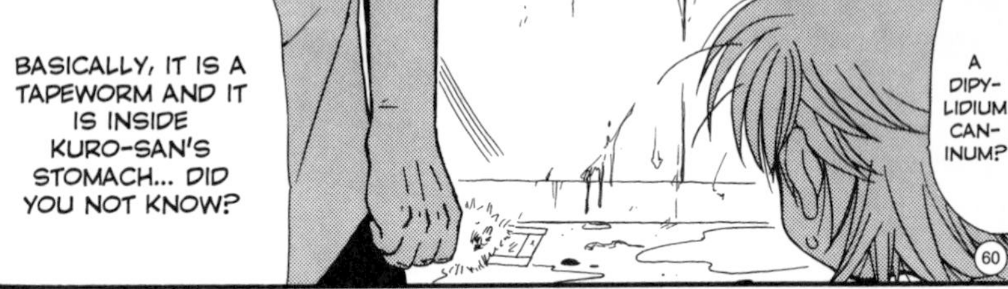
A DIPY-LIDIUM CAN-INUM?
BASICALLY, IT IS A TAPEWORM AND IT IS INSIDE KURO-SAN'S STOMACH... DID YOU NOT KNOW?
60

*EDITOR'S NOTE: VERMIFUGE IS AN AGENT THAT KILLS INTESTINAL WORMS.

61
DID YOU NOT NOTICE THE PROGLOTTIDS AROUND KURO-SAN'S BEHIND?
AND BE CAREFUL. THESE TAPEWORMS CAN ALSO SPREAD TO HUMANS.
ぱッ
ぱッ
......

62
MISATO-SAN HAS BEEN GIVING KURO-SAN FOOD BECAUSE SHE WAS TRYING TO MIX VERMIFUGE* AND HAVE THE CAT TAKE IT THAT WAY.

HMM...
...THERE'S SOME-THING ABOUT THAT CAT...
MISATO-SENPAI...
...SO THAT'S WHAT SHE MEANT BY THAT...

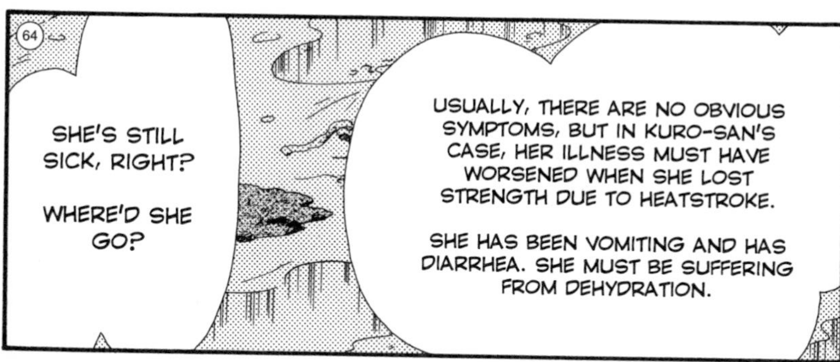
USUALLY, THERE ARE NO OBVIOUS SYMPTOMS, BUT IN KURO-SAN'S CASE, HER ILLNESS MUST HAVE WORSENED WHEN SHE LOST STRENGTH DUE TO HEATSTROKE.
SHE HAS BEEN VOMITING AND HAS DIARRHEA. SHE MUST BE SUFFERING FROM DEHYDRATION.
SHE'S STILL SICK, RIGHT?
WHERE'D SHE GO?

HUH? WHAT'S UP, WATA?
WAS SHE SHARPENING HER NAILS? MAYBE SHE'S NOT AS SICK AS WE THINK...

ANYWAY, I'M GOING TO SCHOOL.

TASUKE, YOU HAVE MISUNDERSTOOD.

ANIMALS SOMETIMES LEAVE SCRATCH MARKS AS A WAY OF EXPRESSING INFORMATION.

THIS MUST BE A MESSAGE KURO-DONO LEFT!

WHAT DOES IT SAY?

"THANK YOU VERY MUCH FOR TAKING CARING OF ME."

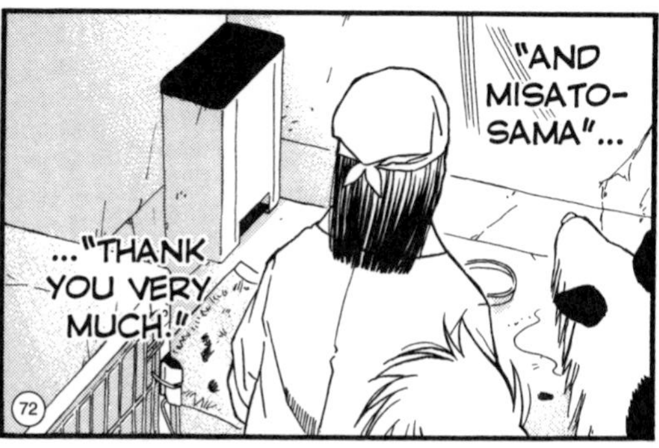
"AND MISATO-SAMA"...
..."THANK YOU VERY MUCH."

ジリ
ジリ

"AND I APOLOGIZE FOR EXPOSING YOU TO DANGER."

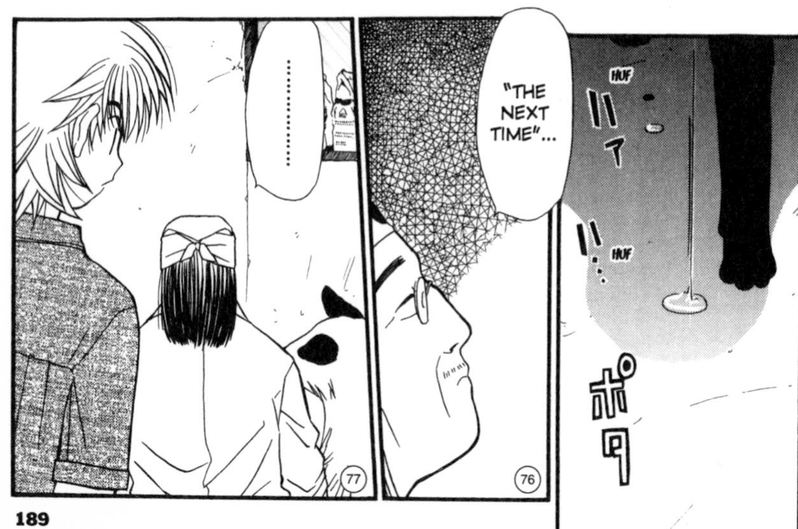
HUF
ハァ
HUF
ハ...
ポタ
"THE NEXT TIME"...
....

78
WHAT, DAD?
"THE NEXT TIME," WHAT?
79
THIS IS...

ぐい
WE DO NOT HAVE TIME!
80
TASUKE, WE MUST FIND HER!
!?

81
KURO-DONO...
...KURO-DONO HAS PREPARED HERSELF FOR DEATH!
82

83
HUF
ハア
ヨロ

84
I'M PROBABLY GOING TO DIE SOON.
BUT THAT'S OK.

85
IF I DIE AND GO AWAY, SO WILL BAD LUCK!
THIS IS THE KIND OF CAT I AM, BUT...

86
"THE NEXT TIME I'M BORN"...

87
88
..."I'LL COME BACK AS A WHITE CAT. SO MISATO-SAMA AND MASTER WATA"...

89
..."PLEASE ALLOW ME TO STAY BY YOUR SIDE THEN."

I DON'T WANT TO MAKE PEOPLE SUFFER ANYMORE!

VOLUME 1
:END.

北斗の拳
www.raijincomics.com
RAIJIN COMICS ™
©1983 Buronson/Hara Tetsuo/Coamix Inc.

Bow Wow Wata, Vol.1

ART & STORY:
UMEKAWA KAZUMI

Editorial Production: Coamix Inc.
Editor: Sam Kondo
Senior Editor: Jonathan Tarbox
Director of Sales: Yamamoto Hideki
Senior Manager, GUTSOON! ENTERTAINMENT: Michael Palmieri
General Manager: Kashimura Yukihiro
Editor-in-Chief: Negishi Tadashi
Publisher: Horie Nobuhiko

Art Direction: SPAZIO ARANCIA
Printing: Toppan Printing Co., (H.K.) Ltd.
Editorial Cooperation: C.P.U.GO
Sakurai Susumu

Published by GUTSOON! ENTERTAINMENT
P.O. Box 14148, Torrance, CA 90503

ISBN: 1-932454-18-7
First Printing, Jan. 2004
10 9 8 7 6 5 4 3 2